$.50
9/22
EH

MAPS IN CONTEXT
A Workbook for American History

Volume 1: To 1877

D0073953

Gerald A. Danzer
University of Illinois at Chicago

Bedford/St. Martin's

Boston ◆ New York

Contents

Introduction

Maps and historical studies have much in common: both use art and science to create representations of things we cannot experience directly. In the case of maps, most spaces are too vast and the geography too complex to be understood with a single look. History has an additional challenge: the past has forever slipped away and we need devices to help us recover and understand it. Both the cartographer (or map maker) and the historian start by gathering facts, but they are quickly overwhelmed with data, presenting the need to select, shorten, and clarify their portrayals. The cartographer turns to symbols and visual images while the historian depends primarily on words and concepts. Working together, the historian and the cartographer combine their talents to craft a coherent narrative about the past.

Our conviction is that encouraging students to think geographically will help them to think historically. And *visa versa*. The ultimate goal of geography and history is the same — both attempt to make connections to larger pictures, to see places and events as part of a greater whole. Although geography and history have separate and distinct modes of explanation, ways of asking questions, and styles of appreciation, they rely on each other to present the most complete story possible.

Thus, to excel as a student of American history, some geography is necessary. This workbook for beginners aims to get you started and to offer encouragement along the way. It uses maps as a natural arena where geography and history come together. Each lesson features an historical map, a selected image of the earth drawn today to help us imagine what the world looked like in the past. As models of reality, historical maps extract certain features for emphasis to make the world intelligible. Above all, historical maps are instructional devices, and the cartographer always follows a lesson plan. One way to begin reading a map is to figure out the purpose of the lesson. Stated another way, there is a teacher behind every map.

While historical maps aim to simplify, they are not simple devices. They are quite complicated in their own way and often remind us of the complexity of the human experience as they try to reduce past events to an orderly picture. Just as students of geography, students of history must be cartographically literate — that is, have the ability to read and understand maps of all types. The plan of this workbook is to provide a series of maps accompanied by worksheets to guide students through American history by developing a geographic context. In the process, cartographic literacy will come naturally and, we trust, so will geographical and historical patterns of thought.

This workbook is organized in three sections. Section one, "Basic Geography," works to establish the geographic context of American history and introduces the core themes of geography – location, place, region, movement, and interaction. Section two, "Mapping America's History," explores in a chronological manner a variety of topics, events, movements, and concepts that are essential parts of the basic structure of any American history course. Section three, "One-Minute Map Quizzes" provides a series of brief quizzes to help you check your knowledge of key places in America's story. The Appendix includes an answer key, and also several American and World outline reference maps.

Every "Basic Geography" and "Mapping America's History" worksheet has three parts. First, "Maptalk" presents a general discussion about the map in its historical context. These introductions are designed to provide a way of thinking about the map in its active teaching role. Second, "Reading the Map" highlights several specific things to look for on the map that will help it become a useful learning device. Third, "Working with the Map," suggests one or more short activities designed to pull it all together. Many of these activities are open-ended with no "correct answers", allowing instructors maximum flexibility to adapt the workbook material to their own teaching style.

More than a collection of exercises focused on a particular area of study, a workbook is connected to an approach to education based on active learning. As a companion to your American history textbook, *Maps in Context* provides a rich collection of hands-on lessons to help you develop your skills in thinking both geographically and historically—and to understand the essential connections between the two. Both are avenues to human understanding and self-awareness. We wish you every success on your journey.

Gerald A. Danzer
University of Illinois at Chicago

SECTION ONE
Basic Geography

The World on a Mercator Projection

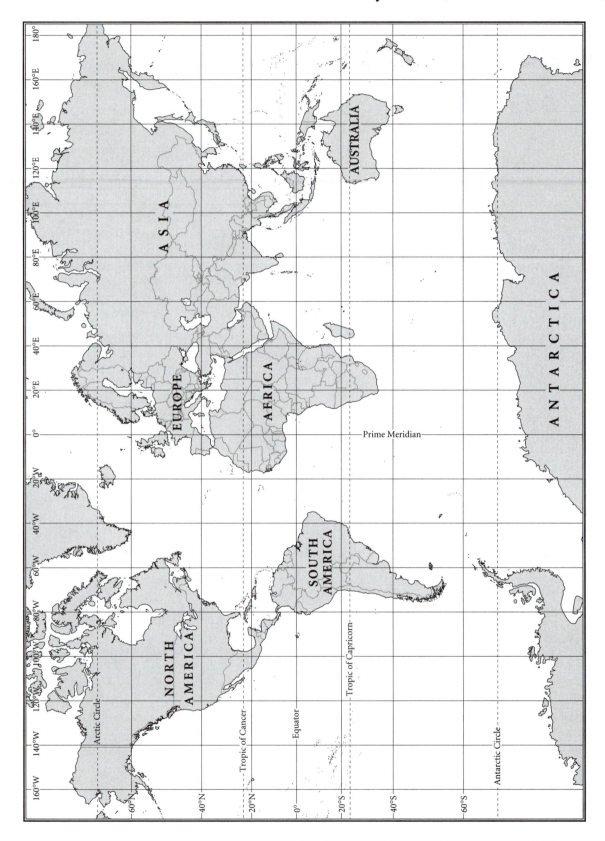

Maptalk: Location

In many ways, all history courses start with a world map. In studying the past to gain some insight into the human condition, a global stage is needed because over thousands of generations humanity has migrated over the earth. This story of migration is especially applicable to American history as it is studied and taught today: a meeting place where various peoples have come together to fashion a new society and culture.

Maps are the best devices to show location, and any place on a map is located in reference to the earth as a whole. Of the many ways in which the earth can be mapped as a complete unit, the Mercator projection is probably the most familiar. A map projection is any technique used to transfer an image of the three-dimensional earth to a two-dimensional sheet of paper. Every approach tries to preserve some feature of the earth's surface, like area, direction, or distance, and in the process distorts others. In 1569 the Flemish cartographer Gerardus Mercator, by trial and error, worked out a formula so that any great circle on the globe would be a straight line on a map. Mercator stretched the map in a way that results in great distortions in distance and area as one proceeds poleward, but preserves true direction. This was a notable achievement in a seafaring society dependent on accurate information for navigation.

The rectangular grid of Mercator's map makes it easy to find locations using a global position of "latitude" and "longitude." Lines of latitude circle the globe east to west and are called *parallels*. Lines of longitude circle the globe north to south and are called *meridians*. This system of lines is sometimes called absolute location. Relative location, thinking about a place in terms of its surroundings rather than its precise site, is also encouraged by the Mercator projection because the directions are always true, running as straight lines on the map. Thus it is easy to see that South America lies considerably east of North America.

Reading the Map

1. Note that the sizes of areas pictured at the top and bottom of the map are quite distorted. Greenland, which looks like a continent on the map, is really less than one-third the size of Australia and less than one-eight the size of South America.

2. The equator spans all the points on the earth's surface that are midway between the poles. Near the equator the sun shines with its greatest strength, making the equatorial regions the hottest climates.

3. The Tropic of Cancer in the Northern Hemisphere and the Tropic of Capricorn in the Southern Hemisphere mark the end of the tropical regions, places where the sun shines directly overhead during the year.

4. The Arctic Circle and the Antarctic Circle, in contrast, mark the beginning of the high latitudes where during the winter, or low-sun season, there is at least one day in which the sun never gets above the horizon.

5. The middle latitudes are found between the polar regions and the tropics. These are regions of temperate climates, usually with distinct seasons like summer and winter, or a dry season and a wet season.

6. By international agreement, the measurement of longitude begins at the prime meridian, 0°. This meridian is a line through the observatory in Greenwich, England, a borough of London.

7. Longitude is measured both east and west of the prime meridian, reaching 180°, halfway around the world. The International Date Line runs near the 180th meridian.

Working with the Map

This exercise will help you review the basic global context for American history. Washington, D.C., has a global position of about 39° N., 77° W. Locate it on the map and extend lines in the cardinal directions (north, south, east, and west) from America's capitol. Which of the following places do these lines cross? Consult a reference atlas and mark "yes" or "no" in the spaces provided.

_____	England	_____	South Africa
_____	Spain	_____	Mexico
_____	China	_____	Canada
_____	Afghanistan	_____	Cuba
_____	Japan	_____	Russia

The World on a Peters Equal-Area Projection

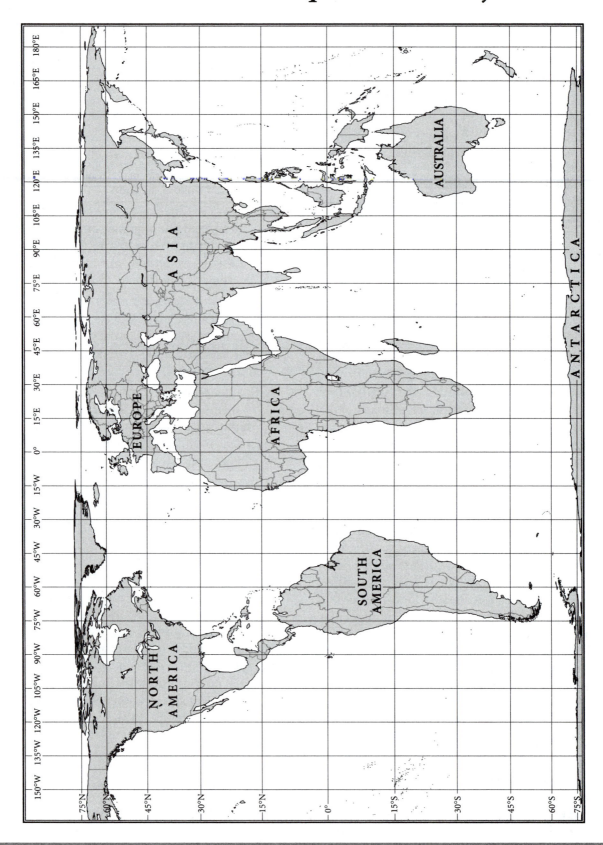

Maptalk: Location

The global position of any place expressed in terms of latitude and longitude is always the same no matter which projection is used. The Mercator projection used in Worksheet A, for example, maintains "true-direction." The one shown here is an "equal-area" presentation, first developed by James Gall in the nineteenth century. In 1973 Arno Peters, a German historian, advocated the use of this type of map to correct the area distortions of the familiar Mercator projection. Peters believed that traditional maps like Mercator's emphasized Europe and the Northern Hemisphere at the expense of the tropical region. His solution was to elongate the low latitudes and flatten the high latitudes. In the process, accuracy of direction, distance, and shape were all compromised, but the projection did show equal areas around the globe.

To correct traditional "eurocentric" maps, Peters designed his projection so that the center of the map was the point where the equator struck the Atlantic coast of Africa, about 10° east of the prime meridian (0 degrees longitude).

Reading the Map

1. The meridians on this map divide the world into twenty-four zones, one for each hour of the day. The prime meridian is set at London and the others are marked off in 15° intervals, roughly reproducing standard time zones.

2. The parallels on this map are not evenly spaced as they would be on a globe, but are adjusted for the curvature of the earth to achieve an equal-area map. Note how the parallels divide the earth into twelve zones between the poles, again set 15° apart.

3. In almost all cylindrical projections, it is very difficult to show the very high latitudes (above 80°) or to indicate the earth's poles. Note how these are flattened on this example.

4. The world's oceans are well presented on this map because it is an equal-area projection. Turning the image upside down with Antarctica at the top will emphasize the dominance of water over land on the earth's surface. Note the continuous water passage at 60° south.

Working with the Map

Because the meridians on this map are parallel it is possible to cut the image along any degree of longitude and move it to the outside edges of the map. Remove this page or make a photocopy of it. Then trim the margin on the left hand side of the map. Next cut the image along the 90th east meridian (at the Ganges Delta between India and Malaya). Move the left part of the map to the right side and tape the two parts together. North America will now be at the center of the image.

Write a caption for this new world map explaining its advantages and disadvantages for students of American history.

North American Rivers and Their Basins

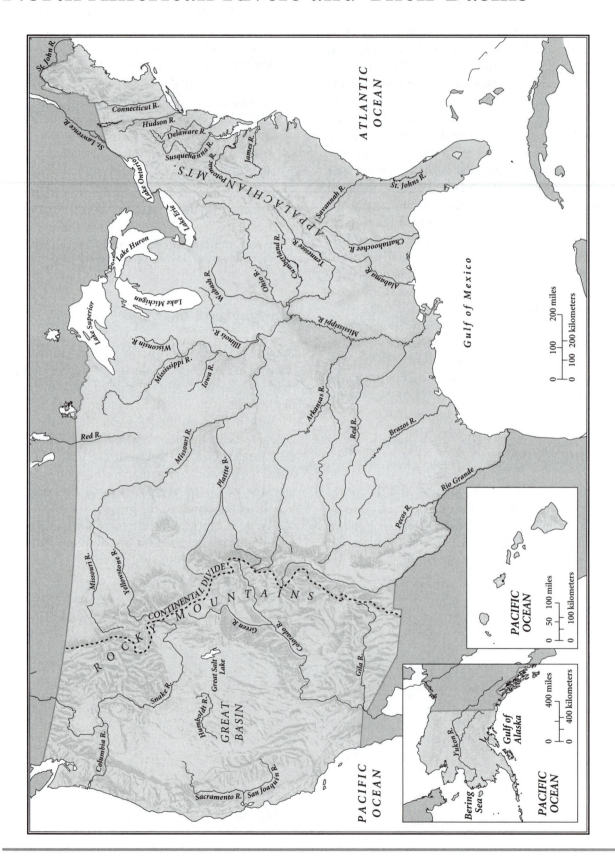

Maptalk: Place

Human activity creates places. Locations exist on their own without the presence of humans, but they become *places* when people use the spot in some way. As generation after generation uses a place, it produces artifacts, develops layers of remains, and accumulates a variety of associations held in a society's memory. At first, human activity may be passive: looking the site over, connecting it to its surroundings, noting its situation, and perhaps giving it a name. Later, humans may start to use the place in some specific way—hunting ground, campsite, field, pasture, settlement, shrine, or pathway. Through use, abstract global positions become specific places of unique character.

Places are usually on land, with readily observed physical characteristics such as topography, soils, and vegetation. Places vary in size. Some, like a field or a town, are assigned certain boundaries by humans. Others, such as rivers and their valleys or basins, are defined by nature. Some places are so circumscribed that they can be perceived at a glance, like the Great Falls of the Snake River. Others, such as the Mississippi Valley, are so vast it would take a lifetime to observe every acre of them.

Places help to give people an identity. Few people think of watersheds—rivers and their basins—when they identify with a particular place, yet rivers and their basins are important to many events in American history. Through the mid-nineteenth century in the era before railroad, highway, and air transportation made water routes less important, access to navigable rivers was crucial to exploration and migration patterns, and to the establishment of towns and cities.

Reading the Map

1. The Continental Divide separates waters flowing into the Atlantic Ocean and those heading toward the Pacific Ocean. Note how the long reach of the Missouri River pushes this line far to the west.

2. The Great Basin has no outlet to the sea. The Great Salt Lake receives much of the run-off in this region, but one river, the Humboldt, drains into a sink long before reaching the salty lake.

3. The Mississippi Valley includes the great river and all its tributaries. Waters from every state between the Appalachians and the Rockies flow toward New Orleans.

4. Many rivers flow from the Appalachian Mountains to the Atlantic, which encouraged the formation of many states along this coast. The Pacific Slope is another story. It has only a few major rivers and only three states.

Working with the Map

On the map draw in the approximate location of the Continental Divide, the extent of the Mississippi Valley, and the reaches of the Great Basin. Use a reference map or atlas to help.

Then locate and identify on the map the following: Niagara Falls, the Grand Canyon, the Falls of St. Anthony, Yellowstone Falls, Hoover Dam, the Mississippi Delta, Lake Okeechobee.

Next locate the following cities on the map and match with their river location.

_____ 1. New York   A. Source of the Ohio River

_____ 2. Denver   B. Near Hoover Dam

_____ 3. Santa Fe   C. Falls of the Ohio River

_____ 4. Minneapolis   D. Delaware River

_____ 5. Kansas City   E. Source of the Platte

_____ 6. Louisville   F. Rio Grande

_____ 7. Philadelphia   G. Mouth of the Hudson

_____ 8. Portland   H. Missouri River

_____ 9. Las Vegas   I. Mouth of the Columbia

_____10. Pittsburgh   J. Mississippi River waterfall

Geography of the United States

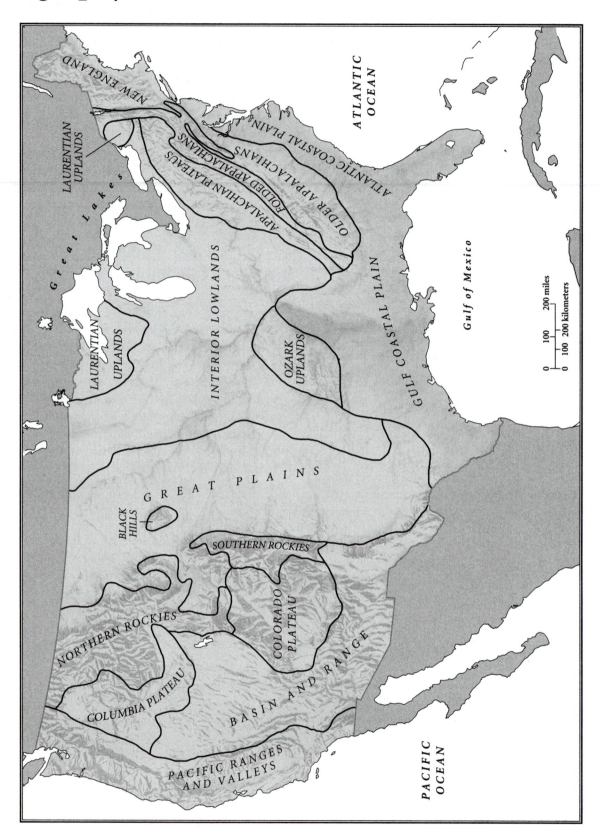

Maptalk: Region

When historians refer to the geographic setting of American history they usually mean the physical character of the land. The actual locations where events "took place" need to be imagined on any historical map. Thus, reference to an event on the Atlantic Coastal Plain, in the Rocky Mountains, or on the Colorado Plateau will spark certain pictorial images or representative landscapes in the reader's mind.

To begin the study of American history, a review of the nation's major physiographic regions is useful. A region is a group of places that share common characteristics that distinguishes them from surrounding areas. For physiographic regions, these distinguishing features are physical characteristics usually related to geological structure and its resulting topography. Thus places with a similar lay of the land, resulting from either physical features (e.g., similar rock formations) or from the experience of a common history, are called regions.

Reading the Map

1. There are several major mountain range systems in the United States. The old Appalachian Uplands extend from Georgia and Alabama north to New York and New England.

2. The Appalachian system is a series of mountains that have been worn down over millennia by erosion. Some are folded mountains resulting from the compression of the land mass. Foothills and extensive plateaus characterize the Appalachians in the east to the Great Lakes and the Ohio Valley in the west.

3. The Midwest, south and west of the Great Lakes, is often called the Interior Lowlands.

4. The Appalachians separate the Atlantic Coastal Plain from the Interior Lowlands, a series of plains that extend across the continent. The Gulf Coastal Plain continues the Atlantic lowland west to Texas where it meets the Great Plains, a higher and drier region that reaches northward to the Arctic Ocean.

5. The mountains of the Great West start with the Rockies, a series of young ranges that rise suddenly from the Great Plains. West of the Rockies are two high plateaus named after their major rivers: the Colorado and the Columbia. Then the extensive Basin and Range area extends from west Texas to California. Most of these dry lands in Nevada and Utah lack an outlet to the sea, resulting in the Great Salt Lake and similar lakes and sinks.

6. A series of high mountain ranges, deep valleys, and lower but very rugged coastal ranges mark the Pacific coast.

Working with the Map

Consult an atlas or a reference map to locate the following places. Then place them on the map and indicate the physiographic region they are associated with.

Place	Region
_____ 1. Grand Canyon	A. Atlantic Coastal Plain
_____ 2. Detroit	B. Appalachian system
_____ 3. Spokane	C. Gulf Coastal Plain
_____ 4. Pittsburgh	D. Interior Lowlands
_____ 5. Wichita	E. Great Plains
_____ 6. Mobile	F. Rocky Mountains
_____ 7. The Chesapeake	G. Columbia Plateau
_____ 8. Death Valley	H. Colorado Plateau
_____ 9. Pike's Peak	I. Basin and Range
_____ 10. The Golden Gate	J. Pacific ranges and valleys

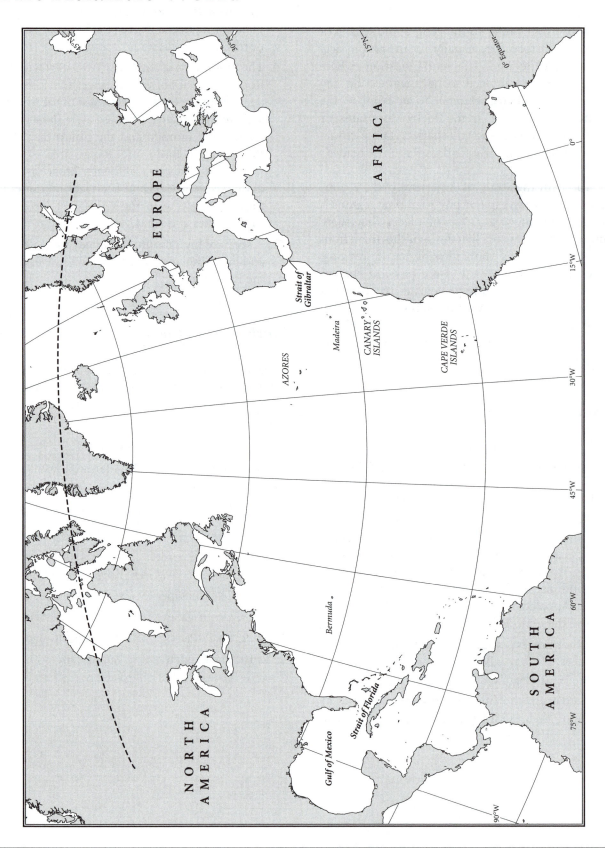

Maptalk: Movement

The concept of an Atlantic World is a key to understanding important topics in American history: the European explorations, the building of overseas empires, the African diasporas resulting from the slave trade, the great migration of peoples from Europe to the New World, the world wars of the twentieth century, and the emergence of a global economy.

The geographic theme of movement lies at the heart of the idea of an Atlantic World. Without movement back and forth across the Atlantic, we would not conceive of a region centered on an ocean. When people first began crossing the Atlantic at the end of the fifteenth century, goods, ideas, beliefs, diseases, plants, and animals traveled with them, in what is termed the "Columbian Exchange." For five centuries, the Atlantic has connected people living along its shores even as it physically separated them. The concept of an Atlantic civilization focuses on the elements connecting Europe, Africa, and the Americas.

Reading the Map

1. The projection used for this map curves both the meridians and the parallels. The result emphasizes the basin-like character of the north Atlantic Ocean.

2. Note the eastward thrust of South America. The distance from Cape Verde on the African coast to the eastern tip of South America is less than 2000 miles.

3. The Gulf of Mexico carries the waters of the Atlantic westward almost to the 98th meridian, more than one-fourth of the way around the globe. It is over 4600 miles from the Strait of Gibraltar to the Strait of Florida.

4. In the age of sail, wind patterns and currents influenced the choice of a trans-Atlantic route. In the air age, however, great circles such as the dotted line between central Europe and the Great Plains became the shortest routes for aircraft. Note how this pathway crosses near Iceland, Greenland, and Hudson Bay on a flight from Warsaw to Denver.

5. Europe is much further north than the Atlantic coast of the United States. Land's End at the southwestern tip of Great Britain is at 50° latitude, 11° north of Washington, D.C.

Working with the Map

To fully comprehend the patterns of European exploration and settlement in the Americas, it is helpful to understand the clockwise motion of major currents of the North Atlantic. The Canary Current starts off the Strait of Gibraltar and reaches the Cape Verde Islands before turning westward as the North Equatorial Current. This steady current is pushed by the trade winds to the West Indies. The Gulf Stream continues the circulation pattern, sending warm tropical waters through the Strait of Florida and along the Carolina coast before cutting across the ocean in a northeasterly direction, reaching from Iceland to Spain as the broad North Atlantic Drift.

Use arrows and labels to indicate the circulation patterns of currents on the map. Then consult a reference atlas and label the following places:

Sahara	Greenland
Brazil	Iceland
Panama	Great Britain
Cuba	France
Newfoundland	Spain
Caribbean Sea	Hudson Bay

Large-Scale Maps

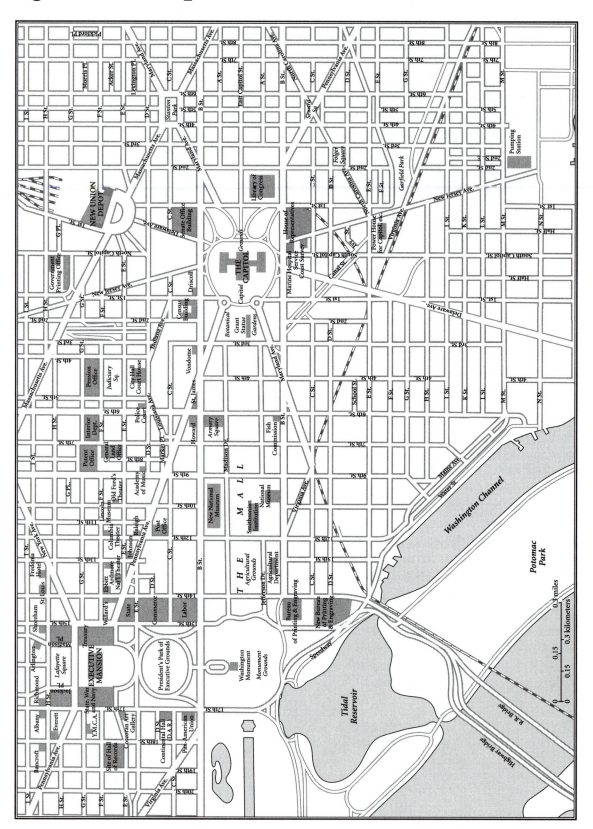

Maptalk: Interaction

A large-scale map, by definition, is one on which individual features are drawn close to the scale used for the map. On this map of Washington, D.C. in 1912, the actual outlines of the large public buildings are set to the scale of the map itself. The scale is large enough to make this possible, hence the designation as a large-scale map.

Similarly, streets and pathways, although somewhat exaggerated in size, bear a resemblance to the space they actually occupy. The importance of streets justifies magnifying their size, especially a map like this one designed to help people find their way around the city.

The large scale of this map also helps us envisage the human-environmental interaction that surrounds and influences all human activities. But on an urban street map like this, it seems like the human presence has completely taken over the natural setting and pushed nature to the margins or confined it to parks and reserves. The map reader must make the effort to keep the natural environment in mind.

Any plan for a settlement of any size shows the human pattern imposed on the land. When studied carefully, a map such as this of Washington, D.C. reveals tension between the natural topography and the geometric pattern of blocks and streets. The presence of waterways reminds readers of the natural setting because the human layout must take into account drainage patterns and tidal flows.

Reading the Map

1. Start your exploration of this map by following the shorelines that mark the boundary between land and water. The Potomac River here is part of the large estuary called Chesapeake Bay. Tidal activity is evident in the Tidal Reservoir, which holds back fresh water pushed into the reservoir with each rising tide.

2. Next, note the street pattern which separates the land into blocks and parcels set aside for public and private use. The Capitol is clearly the central focus of this urban plan because major avenues radiate from it as from the hub of a wheel. Three streets and the Mall run in the cardinal directions and divide the city into quadrants: N.W., N.E., S.W., and S.E.

3. Other major buildings include the Union Depot, which seems to rival the Capitol in size, indicating that the nation in 1912 was still in the railroad era. The Executive Mansion (White House) does not seem so imposing as a building, but the urban plan gives it status as the secondary hub. Other large buildings on the map are devoted to government functions, museum space, and headquarters for organizations.

4. Pennsylvania Avenue connects the Executive Mansion with the Capitol, with the Washington Monument serving as the third point in a large federal triangle. Note how the city planners located the obelisk slightly off center so that people at the Capitol would have an unobstructed view due west into the interior of the continent.

5. The "Mall" or park proceeding west from the Capitol to the Potomac emphasized this westward orientation for the capital city. Note how the Mall was formally subdivided in 1912 into sections used for the public gardens, Armory Square, the Smithsonian Institution, the Agricultural Grounds, and the Monument Grounds.

Working with the Map

A comparison of large-scale maps of a specific place at different time periods would demonstrate how human beings change their patterns of interaction with the landscape. Compare this map of Washington, D.C. in 1912 with a current street map of the nation's capital. Focusing on land and water use, write a paragraph detailing the major changes of the twentieth century. How might these changes be accounted for?

States: Building the Union

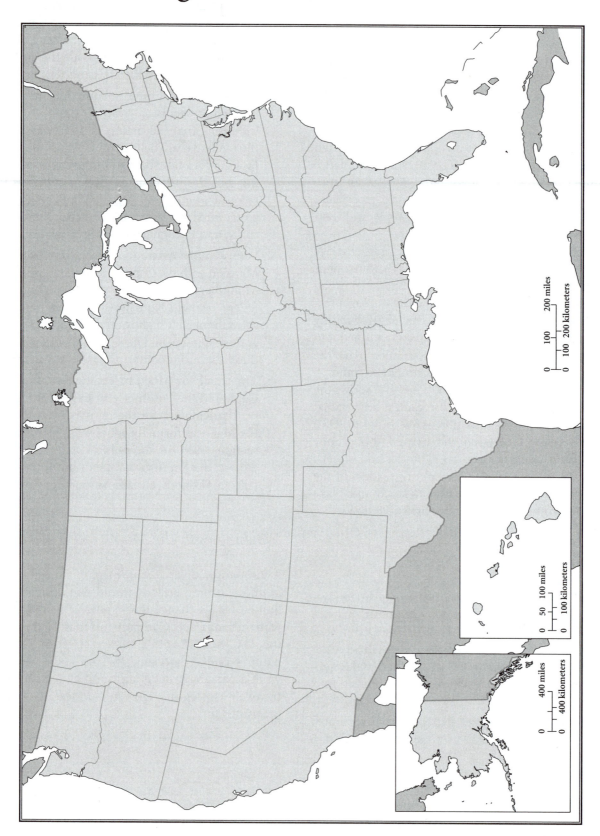

Maptalk: Federal and State

The federal system of United States divides the powers and responsibilities of government between the central government and the states. This division is spelled out in the federal Constitution and in the various state constitutions. Where the separation of powers is not clear, the courts, legislation, and practice all come into play. Any informed discussion of America's past recognizes the importance of elements both of cooperation and tension between states and nation that often surface in political events.

The United States emerged as a nation in the aftermath of the American Revolution—a common struggle for independence by the thirteen British North American colonies. Two types of government resulted: individual independent states and a united confederation. The Declaration of Independence referred to "these united colonies" in advancing their claim to be independent states. The development of the U.S. flag over the years recognized the thirteen original states in the stripes and *all* of the states individually in the stars.

Under the U.S. Constitution, local, state, and federal or central governments have certain powers and responsibilities. International relations are reserved to the federal government. Thus the United States is recognized by other nations as one nation and has only one vote in the United Nations. Local governments are subdivisions of the states, and the placement of local government under the jurisdiction of individual states rather than the central government has brought state government close to the everyday lives of the people.

Reading the Map

1. As the number of states grew new maps had to be created in every decade from the 1790s until 1912. At this point, all the continental territories of the U.S. had become states.

2. The District of Columbia was the only exception to the statement above. Originally part of Maryland, it was ceded to the United States for use as a capital city. Then it became a special district serving as the seat of the federal government.

3. Alaska and Hawaii, which became territories in the later nineteenth century, both became states in 1959. Note how special inset maps with individual scales are needed to include the 49th and 50th states.

4. Some residents of Puerto Rico have advocated statehood for this Caribbean island, but the majority of its people have preferred a commonwealth status instead of either statehood or independence. Puerto Rico does not appear on this map, nor does it get a star on the American flag.

Working with the Map

First test your ability to identify each of the states by placing its name or abbreviation on the map.

Next use a marker to group the states into regional clusters based on their geography and history. The U.S. Census uses nine such categories.

1. New England is made up of the six states within or east of the Connecticut River Valley.

2. The Middle Atlantic states are New York, New Jersey, and Pennsylvania.

3. The South Atlantic states include the states south of Pennsylvania all the way to Florida. West Virginia is included in this group even though it does not touch the Atlantic Ocean.

4. The East North Central states comprise those formed out of the Northwest Territory, except Minnesota.

5. The West North Central states all include territory secured in the Louisiana Purchase: Minnesota, the Dakotas, Iowa, Missouri, Kansas, and Nebraska.

6. The East South Central states are Kentucky, Tennessee, Alabama, and Mississippi, all situated south of the Ohio River.

7. The West South Central states include Texas and three states formed from the Louisiana Purchase: Louisiana, Arkansas, and Oklahoma.

8. The eight Mountain states reach from Mexico to Canada but do not touch the Pacific Ocean.

9. The Pacific states all have long coastlines along the Pacific Ocean: California, Oregon, Washington, Alaska, and Hawaii.

Mapping America's History

Native American Peoples, 1492

Dominant Economic Activity
- Agriculture
- Hunting
- Hunting-gathering
- Fishing

Maptalk

Maps always simplify reality in an effort to convey specific information or to make a point, and this map provides a good example. First, note that the title indicates the major theme of the map, a picture of Native American peoples in 1492. But only a fraction of the many peoples are named on the map. In the California region, for example, there were about 500 distinct peoples in 1492, but only three are noted. Therefore this map simplifies reality by selection.

The map divides the land into four major categories by dominant economic activity, a process of simplification by generalization. To say that agriculture or hunting or fishing was the dominant economic activity in any particular region is to make a statement which is generally true, but often qualified by the varied activities of a particular group or by the time of the year. To make their maps legible, cartographers use broad categories and general statements; their maps would be too crowded and complicated if every situation was given equal consideration.

The scale in the lower left illustrates another way maps are often simplified: scales reduce real distances to a fraction of reality. In this case, one inch on the page equals 800 miles on the ground. Topography can only be suggested. Individual mountain peaks cannot be shown in this scale; neither can all the major rivers and lakes be pictured. Every time you "map something out," a process of simplification is at work.

Reading the Map

1. Note that this map covers all of North America because the Native American peoples occupied every region from the islands of the Arctic Ocean to the Isthmus of Panama.

2. For centuries before 1492 various native peoples had settled all of the habitable islands in the Caribbean Sea.

3. The peopling of America extends to Tierra Del Fuego in the southern reaches of the Western Hemisphere (not depicted). The history of humans in North and South America may extend back twenty millennia.

4. The site of the earliest recorded contact between peoples of the Old and New Worlds, about the year 1000 A.D., was in Newfoundland, called Vinland by the early sagas or stories.

5. The date of this map, 1492, refers to the first voyage of Christopher Columbus. He and his crew met Native Americans on several small islands in the Caribbean as well as on Cuba and Hispaniola.

Working with the Map

At first glance, this map may appear to be static, like a snapshot in which everyone and everything is at rest. Looking at the map with historical eyes, however, brings a dynamic sense of movement to the map. History is the study of change over time, and the locations of peoples on this map should be understood as a pause in a long-term historical process of migration that would continue into the future. With your textbook and/or an historical atlas as your guide, draw arrows on the map to trace the following movements of peoples, using different colors to distinguish each group.

1. Migration of various peoples from northeast Asia at the time of the great ice sheets.

2. The long trek of the Navajo peoples from their ancestral home between Hudson Bay and the Mackenzie River to the region which is now Arizona and New Mexico.

3. The ventures of the Vikings from Iceland (off the map to the east) to Greenland and Vinland (Newfoundland)

4. The first voyage of Columbus and his fleet in 1492, which contacted native peoples in the Bahama Islands, Cuba, and Hispaniola.

Eastern North America in 1650

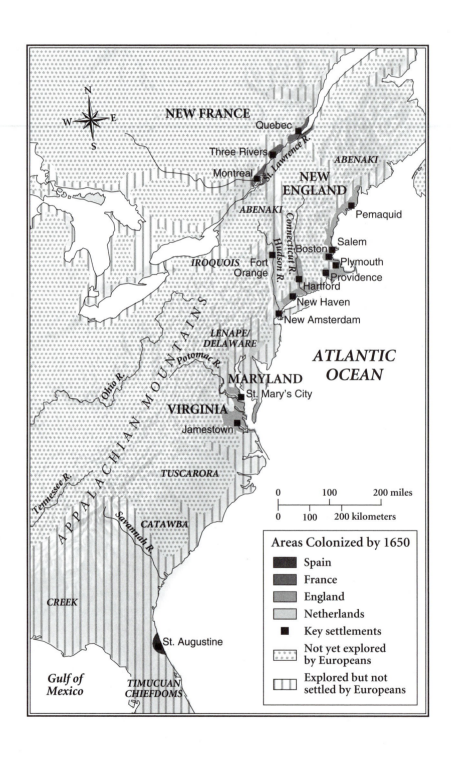

NEW FRANCE
Quebec
Three Rivers
Montreal
St. Lawrence R.
ABENAKI
NEW ENGLAND
ABENAKI
Pemaquid
Connecticut R.
Salem
Hudson R.
Boston
Plymouth
IROQUOIS Fort Orange
Providence
Hartford
New Haven
New Amsterdam
LENAPE/ DELAWARE
ATLANTIC OCEAN
Potomac R.
Ohio R.
APPALACHIAN MOUNTAINS
MARYLAND
St. Mary's City
VIRGINIA
Jamestown
Tennessee R.
TUSCARORA
Savannah R.
CATAWBA
CREEK
St. Augustine
Gulf of Mexico
TIMUCUAN CHIEFDOMS

0   100   200 miles
0   100   200 kilometers

Areas Colonized by 1650
- Spain
- France
- England
- Netherlands
- ■ Key settlements
- Not yet explored by Europeans
- Explored but not settled by Europeans

Maptalk

This map shows coastal North America north to south from the Gulf of St. Lawrence to the Gulf of Mexico. The Atlantic Coastal Plain narrows as the Appalachian Mountains veer toward the northeast, pinching off the flat lands where the Hudson River reaches the sea.

In 1650 most of the coastal plain remained in the hands of Native Americans, although the ravages of new diseases had already disrupted aboriginal peoples. No European settlement extended inland very far from the avenues of ocean-going commerce. On the southern Atlantic coast, the Spanish settlement at St. Augustine was a northern outpost of a widespread empire reaching from the Gulf of Mexico through South America.

Further north, in the Chesapeake region, by mid-century the English established the colonies of Virginia and Maryland. Along the Hudson River, the Dutch erected trading posts at New Amsterdam (later New York) and Fort Orange. To the north, on the New England coast the English Puritans founded a series of colonies focused on port settlements, most notably Boston, New Haven, and Salem. From these harbors ships kept the New World in contact with the Old.

Among the Europeans, the French by way of the St. Lawrence River, pushed furthest into the heart of North America but were stopped at the gateway to the Great Lakes by the Iroquois Confederacy. Thus, Atlantic America in 1650 consisted of a series of distinct colonial outposts, each one connected to the sea and surrounded by territories controlled by Native American peoples.

Reading the Map

1. Note that in 1650 the western Great Lakes remained unexplored by Europeans.
2. Although the Ohio and Tennessee Rivers are labeled on the map, the Mississippi Valley, the great basin which anchors the middle of the continent, was beyond the control of the European colonists.
3. In 1650, Hartford was the single inland colonial settlement and could be reached either by ascending the Connecticut River or by trails that crossed the dense forests from Providence, Plymouth, and Boston. The future development of these pathways into primitive roads helped to create a strong sense of region in New England.
4. France was the first colonial power to penetrate the American interior by way of the St. Lawrence River and its tributaries. Several portages enabled French explorers seeking furs and missionaries in search of souls to reach the straits, which connect lakes Huron, Superior, and Michigan. From there, expeditions like those of Marquette and Joliet (1673) made the vast extent of the Mississippi Valley known to European geographers.

Working with the Map

Developing some knowledge of the expansion of European colonies in North America pushes the reader to set the map in motion. To begin building a sense of the sequence in which some colonial outposts were founded, use a red pen to write the date of settlement of the following locations on the map. Proceed in chronological order. For settlements founded after 1650, consult a reference atlas to find their locations and add these names and dates to the map as well.

1. St. Augustine, 1565
2. Jamestown, 1607
3. Quebec, 1608
4. Fort Orange, 1624
5. New Amsterdam, 1626
6. Boston, 1630
7. St. Mary's City, 1634
8. Hartford, 1636
9. Montreal, 1642
10. Wilmington, North Carolina 1665
11. Mission at Sault Ste. Marie, 1668
12. Charleston, South Carolina, 1670
13. Philadelphia, 1681

Africa and the Eighteenth-Century Atlantic Slave Trade

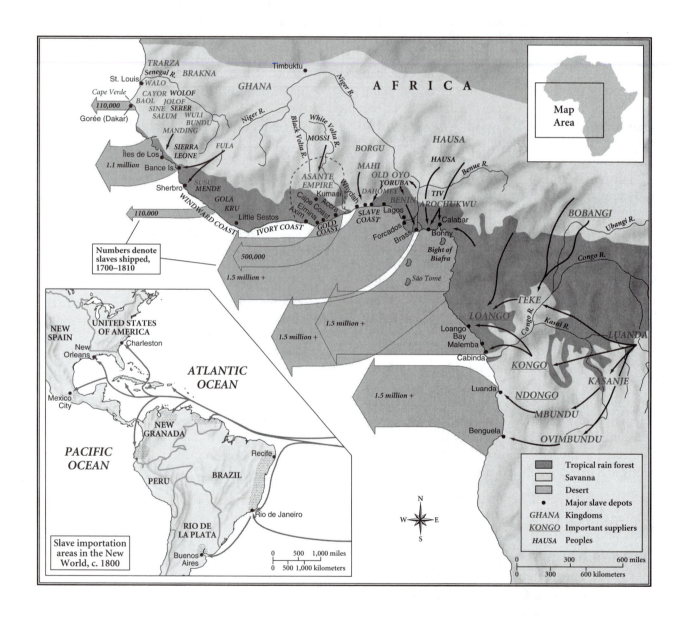

Maptalk

Movement, one of the five major themes of geography, always involves two or more places. As people, goods, and ideas move across space, several maps may be needed to develop a full understanding of the historical processes. Note that the two slave-trade maps provided here show places of origin in the Old World and places of destination in the New. The cartographer assumes that the reader has in mind the map of the Atlantic world, the site of the Middle Passage between Africa and the Americas. (Remember that Worksheet E reviewed this basic geography.)

Reading the Map

1. The upper right of the large map shows that the homelands for most slaves sent to America were in West Africa. A small percentage of slaves also came from the eastern and southern parts of the continent, areas not included on the main map.

2. The first set of arrows indicates that most slaves came from the interior, far from coastal areas. Captives seized in the interior were marched to the coastal ports. Here, African slave traders dealt their human goods to European merchants.

3. The second set of arrows, showing the crossing of the ocean, also serves as a graph indicating the number of slaves sent from slaving stations along the West African coast. The wider the arrow is, the greater the number of slaves who made the Middle Passage.

4. The map of the Americas shows the slave importing areas in the New World. Most slaves were used as agricultural laborers on plantations in Brazil and the Caribbean.

5. Note that in 1800 Florida was not part of the United States. It was a Spanish colony.

Working with the Map

West African cultures relied on strong oral traditions. People used various memory aids, like key words, to help keep records. Imagine yourself a young man captured in the interior of Africa in 1750 who found himself on a South Carolina rice plantation six months later. What key words would he use to help him remember the various segments of his horrific half-year?

Segment of Journey	Key Words

European Spheres of Influence, 1754

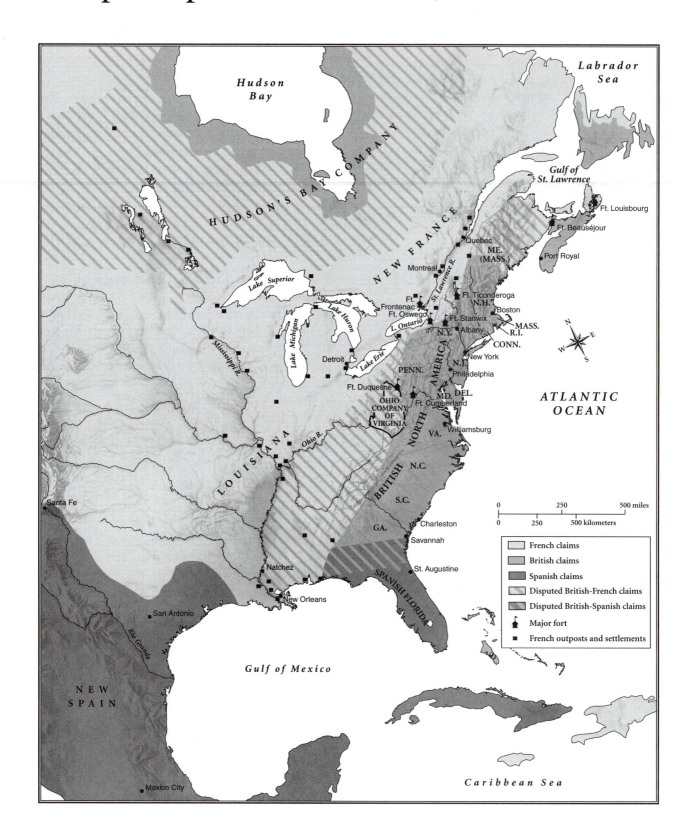

Hudson Bay

Labrador Sea

HUDSON'S BAY COMPANY

NEW FRANCE

Gulf of St. Lawrence

Ft. Louisbourg

Ft. Beauséjour

Quebec

ME. (MASS.)

Port Royal

Montreal

Lake Superior

Ft. Ticonderoga

N.H.

Ft. Frontenac

St. Lawrence R.

Ft. Oswego

Boston

Lake Huron

Ft. Stanwix

MASS.

Lake Michigan

L. Ontario

Albany

R.I.

N.Y.

CONN.

Detroit

Lake Erie

New York

Mississippi R.

PENN.

N.J.

Philadelphia

NORTH AMERICA

Ft. Duquesne

MD. DEL.

OHIO COMPANY OF VIRGINIA

Ft. Cumberland

LOUISIANA

Ohio R.

VA.

Williamsburg

BRITISH

ATLANTIC OCEAN

N.C.

Santa Fe

S.C.

GA.

Charleston

Savannah

Natchez

SPANISH FLORIDA

St. Augustine

New Orleans

San Antonio

Rio Grande

NEW SPAIN

Gulf of Mexico

Mexico City

Caribbean Sea

0		250		500 miles
0	250		500 kilometers	

Legend:
- French claims
- British claims
- Spanish claims
- Disputed British-French claims
- Disputed British-Spanish claims
- Major fort
- French outposts and settlements

Maptalk

A "sphere of influence" refers to the general area in which a political entity is able to establish or maintain its dominance. This dominance might be exercised through military or economic power, but in eighteenth century international law it rested on formal claims made by the mother country and the extent to which other states and empires recognized these claims.

The boundaries of these spheres of influence were often vague, imprecise, and overlapping. Vast territories were often in dispute between two or more imperial powers. Boundary lines on the map may look very precise, but in reality one empire met another on a broad frontier where the limits of actual influences were undefined. Loyalties in these areas shifted and changed frequently. Thus, maps like this one, showing the political situation in North America in 1754, have a very tentative character. The cross-shaded areas indicate the extent of disputed areas. Political dominance in these disputed areas rested with no single power, and was in constant flux.

Reading the Map

1. Note that three major imperial powers laid claim to most of North America in 1754. The boundaries between these claims were often disputed.
2. Spanish holdings in North America centered on New Spain and various islands in the Caribbean. Three important frontier outposts are shown on this map: Santa Fe, at the headwaters of the Rio Grande; San Antonio on the Great Plains; and St. Augustine at the head of the Florida Peninsula.
3. The British colonies extended along the Atlantic coast north of Florida from Georgia to the Gulf of St. Lawrence. In addition, England's Hudson's Bay Company claimed a vast area in the far north.
4. France's North American empire in 1754 included a few claims in the Caribbean region, but centered on two great basins which drain the continent's interior: the Great Lakes-St. Lawrence River and the Mississippi Valley. Montreal and New Orleans were the two great anchors for this vast empire.
5. The Ohio River valley became the site of greatest tension between British and French imperial claims. In 1754, the British Ohio Company of Virginia was set to push settlements across the Appalachian Mountains, but newly erected French forts in the upper reaches of the valley slowed British plans. France's Fort Duquesne occupied the key site where the Allegheny and Monongahela Rivers joined to form the Ohio.

Working with the Map

This map helps readers grasp the difficulties imperial centers faced in communicating with their outposts in their various spheres of influence. In the mid-eighteenth century, before the invention of the telegraph, telephone, or the Internet, most communication required direct person-to-person contact. Use the map to trace the probable routes for land or water communication between the places listed on the chart. Use a different color for each route and suggest a name for the artery on the key below.

Name of Route	Places Connected	Color
1.	Philadelphia and Boston	
2.	Mexico City and Santa Fe	
3.	Montreal and the mouth of the Ohio River	
4.	New Orleans and Green Bay	
5.	St. Augustine and San Antonio	
6.	Williamsburg and Savannah	

British Western Policy, 1763–1774

HUDSON'S BAY COMPANY

Gulf of
St. Lawrence

Louisbourg

Quebec

(MASS.)

Port Royal

Montreal

Lake Superior

St. Lawrence R.

N.H.

(VIRGINIA)

Lake Michigan

Lake Huron

Lake Ontario

NEW
YORK MASS.

Boston

Albany

CONN.

SPANISH LOUISIANA

(VIRGINIA AND MASS.)

Lake Erie

R.I.

PENN.

New York

Philadelphia

N.J.

(VIRGINIA AND CONN.)

ATLANTIC
OCEAN

(VIRGINIA)

MD.

DEL.

Ohio R.

VANDALIA

VIRGINIA

TRANSYLVANIA

Mississippi R.

NORTH CAROLINA

SOUTH
CAROLINA

Charleston

GEORGIA

(CLAIMED BY SPAIN
AND GEORGIA)

Gulf of Mexico

50°N

40°N

30°N

90°W

80°W

70°W

| 0 | 150 | 300 miles |
| 0 | 150 | 300 kilometers |

**Boundaries after
Treaty of Paris, 1763**

British trading company
British colonies
Spain
Quebec in 1763
Quebec in 1774
Proclamation Line of 1763
State boundaries including
western claims
Proposed western colonies

Maptalk

Government policy, a course of action to guide current and future decisions selected from several alternatives, often has a spatial dimension. Maps are essential tools of government policy studies. In the case of colonial North America, British imperial authorities commissioned huge, detailed maps and atlases to help in their deliberations. This modern map illustrates the decisions resulting from policies made in London for the entire empire and implemented by officials in several colonies to promote westward expansion.

Colonial charters usually established western boundary lines. Some of these early documents extended the English colonies across the continent. By 1763 the Mississippi River was the commonly accepted western border of British possessions. The British acquisition of French territories in North America as a result of the Seven Years' War resolved imperial struggles over North American lands. In addition, Britain acquired Florida from Spain, reducing friction on the Georgia-Florida frontier. Spain did, however, retain some claims east of the Mississippi River.

These shifting claims and boundaries in North America between 1763 and 1774 created uncertainty and ambiguity, a situation ripe for misunderstanding, conflict, and eventually revolt as imperial policies clashed with colonial interests. Once again, one sees that when viewed carefully the static appearance of a historical map may reveal underlying tensions seen by an informed observer.

Reading the Map

1. Note that the territory controlled by the Hudson's Bay Company included most of the land drained by rivers flowing northward into the bay itself or the Arctic Ocean.

2. The Proclamation Line of 1763 implemented British policy for control of the lands acquired from France in the Peace of Paris that concluded the Seven Years' War. The proclamation organized Quebec and Florida as English colonies, placed all trade with the Indians under royal control, and drew a line along the crest of the Appalachian Mountains to separate the seaboard colonies from lands reserved for the Native Americans.

3. The Quebec Act of 1774 placed the "Indian Reserve" north of the Ohio River as well as the entire Great Lakes Basin under the jurisdiction of Quebec, essentially canceling the claims of the seaboard colonies to these interior lands.

4. Vandalia was a proposed new colony in the American interior sponsored by British investors between 1770 and 1773. A charter for the new venture was drawn up in 1773, but it was never put into effect because of the imperial crisis in the same year initiated by the Boston Tea Party.

Working with the Map

In the space below, write a paragraph as a caption for this map explaining the purpose and results of the Proclamation Line of 1763 and the Quebec Act of 1774. How did these documents reflect British imperial policy and challenge the aspirations of the American seaboard colonies?

New Spain's Northern Empire, 1763–1800

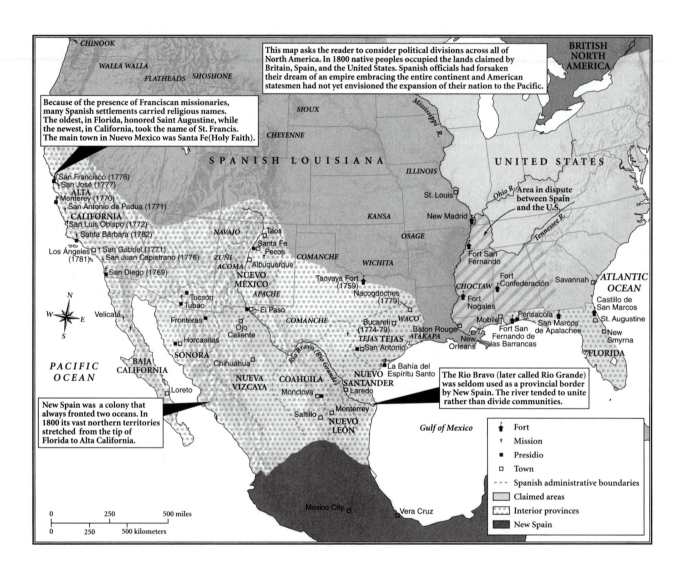

CHINOOK

WALLA WALLA

FLATHEADS   SHOSHONE

BRITISH NORTH AMERICA

This map asks the reader to consider political divisions across all of North America. In 1800 native peoples occupied the lands claimed by Britain, Spain, and the United States. Spanish officials had forsaken their dream of an empire embracing the entire continent and American statesmen had not yet envisioned the expansion of their nation to the Pacific.

Because of the presence of Franciscan missionaries, many Spanish settlements carried religious names. The oldest, in Florida, honored Saint Augustine, while the newest, in California, took the name of St. Francis. The main town in Nuevo Mexico was Santa Fe(Holy Faith).

SIOUX

CHEYENNE

Mississippi R.

SPANISH LOUISIANA

UNITED STATES

ILLINOIS

St. Louis

San Francisco (1776)
San José (1777)
ALTA
Monterey (1770)
San Antonio de Padua (1771)
CALIFORNIA
San Luis Obispo (1772)
Santa Bárbara (1782)
Los Ángeles   San Gabriel (1771)
(1781)   San Juan Capistrano (1776)
San Diego (1769)

NAVAJO   Taos
Santa Fe
Pecos
ZUÑI   Albuquerque
ACOMA
NUEVO
MÉXICO
APACHE
El Paso

COMANCHE

WICHITA

KANSA

OSAGE

New Madrid

Ohio R. Area in dispute between Spain and the U.S.

Tennessee R.

Fort San Fernando

CHOCTAW   Fort Confederación   Savannah   ATLANTIC OCEAN

Castillo de San Marcos
St. Augustine

Taovaya Fort (1759)
Nacogdoches (1779)

Fort Nogales

Tucson
Tubac

Velicatá

Fronteras

Ojo Caliente

Horcasitas

SONORA

Chihuahua

COMANCHE

Bucareli (1774-79)
TEJAS TEJAS
San Antonio

WACO
ATAKAPA
Baton Rouge

Mobile
New Orleans

Pensacola
Fort San Fernando de las Barrancas

San Marcos de Apalachee
New Smyrna

FLORIDA

PACIFIC OCEAN

BAJA CALIFORNIA

Loreto

Rio Bravo (Rio Grande)

NUEVA VIZCAYA

COAHUILA
Monclova

Saltillo

NUEVO SANTANDER
Laredo

Monterrey
NUEVO LEÓN

La Bahía del Espíritu Santo

NUEVO

Gulf of Mexico

The Rio Bravo (later called Rio Grande) was seldom used as a provincial border by New Spain. The river tended to unite rather than divide communities.

New Spain was a colony that always fronted two oceans. In 1800 its vast northern territories stretched from the tip of Florida to Alta California.

Mexico City

Vera Cruz

✚	Fort
†	Mission
■	Presidio
▫	Town
- - -	Spanish administrative boundaries
	Claimed areas
	Interior provinces
	New Spain

N   W   E   S

0   250   500 miles

0   250   500 kilometers

Maptalk

Historical maps often reveal both physical movement and political change over time. Here we examine a map of the Spanish Empire in the late eighteenth century. For the Spanish, the main direction of activity was south to north. Voyages from Vera Cruz sailed north across the Gulf of Mexico to New Orleans and other Spanish settlements along the Gulf coast. The Spanish fleet on the Pacific sailed north along the coast before crossing the ocean to the Philippines. The Mississippi provided a water route north into the American interior. Royal highways starting in Mexico facilitated overland travel north to San Antonio, Santa Fe, and Monterey. A major theme of the continent's history emerged as Spanish, and later Mexican, interests which were oriented northward clashed with the east to west advance of the British and later the Americans.

In Florida, the territorial ambitions of the Spanish Empire and those of the British, followed by the Americans, clashed head-on. Spain lost East and West Florida to the British in the Peace of Paris of 1763, which ended the Seven Years' War, but regained them in the Treaty of Paris of 1783, which concluded the American Revolution. In 1803 the United States purchased from France the Louisiana territory, which included some former Spanish territory. After gradual losses to the Americans, in 1819 Spain ceded the remaining Florida territory to the United States.

Reading the Map

1. Pushed out of the Illinois territory gained by the British, French traders established St. Louis in 1764, in Louisiana, then a Spanish territory. This new trading post on the west bank of the Mississippi later became the gateway to the west for the United States.

2. Santa Fe, founded by the Spanish in 1610, grew into the center of Spanish interests in the American interior. A royal highway, not shown on the map, connected it with Mexico City. A frontier trail later linked Santa Fe and the Mississippi Valley, extending all the way to St. Louis. In the eighteenth century another Spanish trail led westward from Santa Fe to the California missions.

3. New Orleans started as a French trading post in 1718 but came under Spanish rule between 1763 and 1803. Even when it was sold to the United States it retained its Latin character and became the new nation's most picturesque city.

4. In 1691 Spanish missionaries set up a cross near an old Indian settlement and renamed it San Antonio. In 1718 a mission, later known as the Alamo, was built, soon followed by a military post and a settlement of immigrants from the Canary Islands.

5. San Francisco, originally called Yerba Buena, dates from 1776. The Gold Rush of 1849 transformed the sleepy outpost into a bustling city.

Working with the Map

Every fort, mission, presidio, or town named on this map, with the exception of Savannah, has its roots in the Spanish Empire. Select one of these places now in the United States and do some library research on its origins. Then write a caption for the map that emphasizes the local situation in the period 1763–1800. Add some details to the map showing how the place you selected was connected to other places on the map and to the larger context of American history.

The Confederation and Western Land Claims, 1781–1802

Maptalk

This complicated map focuses on a brief but very important period in United States history. It shows the process by which the federal government of the United States, under the Articles of Confederation and then the Constitution, acquired its major asset: millions of acres between the Appalachian Mountains and the Mississippi River formerly claimed by the colonies. The sale of these lands yielded a steady source of income for the national treasury and their development was the engine that drove the economic growth of the new nation.

Virginia ceded the most land, but until the addition of Texas in 1845 remained by far the largest state, with both an extended coastline along Chesapeake Bay and major frontage on the Ohio River. New York and Pennsylvania retained lands that stretched from the Atlantic to the Great Lakes, giving both states a major interest in the development of the American interior. For the smaller states without western land claims like Delaware and New Jersey, the acquisition of the western land by the federal government was a way to share national resources equitably. One commentator referred to the transfer of the western lands to federal ownership as "the cement of the Union."

Reading the Map

1. After the American Revolution, the situation in Vermont was tense as two factions vied for control, one supported the claims of New York and the other proclaimed the area an independent republic. Vermont was admitted to the United States in 1791, but only after sending a delegation to London to inquire about British support for their continued independence.

2. Although Kentucky and Tennessee were, in effect, ceded to the United States by Virginia and North Carolina respectively, these lands did not become federal territory because Congress quickly admitted the two regions as states in 1792 and 1796.

3. Ohio was the first state to go through a territorial period when its lands were sold by the federal government to prospective settlers after the Indian claims to the land had been extinguished by treaties. Ohio became a state in 1803.

Working with the Map

The Northwest Ordinance of 1787 created the Northwest Territory and established a process for its orderly transformation from wilderness to statehood. The legislation established provisions for territorial governments, prohibited slavery, provided for public education, and specified the number of states that could be created out of the territory. Refer to a reference atlas and draw in the boundaries. On the chart below, record the name of the states, date of admission, and note whether it fronts on the Great Lakes, Mississippi River, or Ohio River.

State	Date of Admission	Does the state front on:		
		Great Lakes	Mississippi River	Ohio River
1.				
2.				
3.				
4.				
5.				
6.				

Defining the National Boundaries, 1800–1820

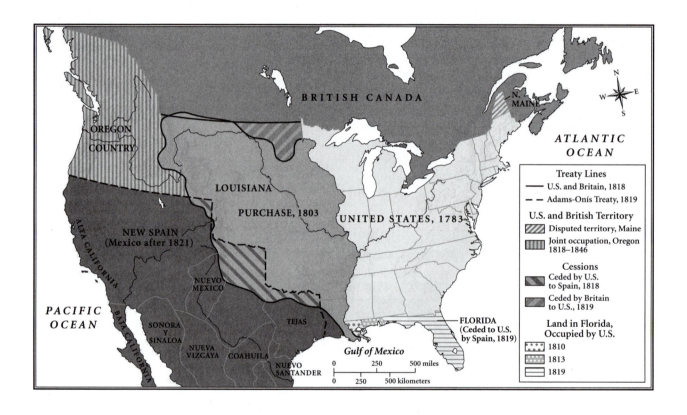

Treaty Lines
— U.S. and Britain, 1818
- - Adams-Onís Treaty, 1819

U.S. and British Territory
Disputed territory, Maine
Joint occupation, Oregon 1818–1846

Cessions
Ceded by U.S. to Spain, 1818
Ceded by Britain to U.S., 1819

Land in Florida, Occupied by U.S.
1810
1813
1819

Maptalk

Maps often divide areas into different categories. This political map focuses on national boundaries and the continent is divided into three major groupings (1) Canada, or British North America, (2) the United States, and (3) New Spain, later Mexico. In addition, the map shows two areas that changed hands during the period under consideration, Louisiana and Florida. The Oregon Country and the disputed territory along Maine's northern border complete the map.

The cartographer has also included the names of the northern provinces of New Spain, a reminder that in 1821 these territories would become part of a newly independent Mexico. The extension of the Spanish frontier northward led to the creation of a separate commander-general for the northern provinces of New Spain in 1776. Louisiana and Florida were also administered separately as individual Spanish provinces until these lands were acquired by the United States in the early nineteenth century.

Tense relations between British Canada and the United States after 1800 culminated in the War of 1812. Peace was restored when the combatants agreed to honor the prewar boundaries. Britain and America avoided further combat and achieved resolution of disputes, such as those over ownership of the Oregon Country.

Reading the Map

1. The Louisiana Purchase dramatically transformed the United States; the size of the Union doubled when these new lands were added in 1803.

2. The Adams-Oñis Treaty of 1819 is sometimes called the Transcontinental Treaty because it settled points of dispute between the United States and Spain from Florida to the Oregon Country. Florida was ceded to the U.S., a boundary was set between New Spain and Louisiana, and Spain gave up its claims to the Oregon Territory when its southern boundary was established at the 42nd parallel.

3. In 1818, the United States and Great Britain agreed to use the 49th parallel as the southern boundary of Canada between the Lake of the Woods and the Rocky Mountains. The Maine boundary was not agreed upon until 1842, and the Oregon dispute was settled in 1846.

4. The United States admitted Louisiana as a state in 1812. Louisiana received some additional territory in 1819 as a result of the Adams-Oñis Treaty.

Working with the Map

Develop an outline for a newspaper editorial on the "Future of the Nation" for publication on January 1, 1820. Base your argument on the events of the past two decades and extend your predictions up to 1840. A map similar to this one will accompany your article. In the space below list three ways you expect the map to change by 1840.

Expected Changes on the Map of North America 1820–1840
1.
2.
3.

WORKSHEET 9
The Missouri Compromise, 1820–1821

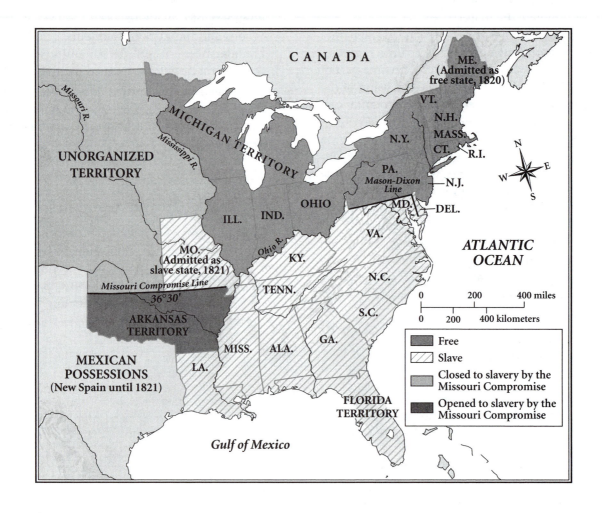

CANADA

ME.
(Admitted as
free state, 1820)

VT.

N.H.

MASS.

N.Y.

CT.

R.I.

MICHIGAN TERRITORY

Missouri R.

Mississippi R.

UNORGANIZED
TERRITORY

PA.
Mason-Dixon
Line

N.J.

OHIO

MD.

DEL.

ILL.

IND.

VA.

Ohio R.

MO.
(Admitted as
slave state, 1821)

KY.

ATLANTIC
OCEAN

Missouri Compromise Line

36°30'

TENN.

N.C.

ARKANSAS
TERRITORY

S.C.

MEXICAN
POSSESSIONS
(New Spain until 1821)

MISS.

ALA.

GA.

LA.

200   400 miles

0

0   200   400 kilometers

FLORIDA
TERRITORY

Free

Slave

Closed to slavery by the
Missouri Compromise

Opened to slavery by the
Missouri Compromise

Gulf of Mexico

Maptalk

To fully comprehend this map some counting is necessary. Both states and organized territories are labeled. The states and territories are further divided into two categories: free and slave. Although slavery was permitted in some fashion in all of the original thirteen colonies and remnants of the institution still existed in some of the "free states," by 1820 it was clear that the Union broke down into two types of states, free and slave.

Because each state held two seats in the U.S. Senate regardless of population, great care was taken to evenly balance the number of free and slave states. This balancing was the essence of the national political compromise that dated back to the drafting of the Constitution, where the proponents of slavery insisted on equal representation in the Senate as the price of union. The balance ensured that Congress could not legislate against their "peculiar institution." Of the original thirteen states, seven eventually became free and six remained slave. Of the three new states admitted to the Union in the 1790s, Vermont was free while Kentucky and Tennessee permitted slavery. When Ohio became a state in 1804, Congress balanced it by adding Louisiana in 1812. The rhythm continued: Indiana entered as a free state in 1816 followed in 1817 by Mississippi as a slave state. Shortly after, Illinois and Alabama entered the Union as a similar match. But Missouri's application to be admitted as a slave state posed a problem. There was no free state waiting in line to maintain the balance. The solution was the Missouri Compromise. The District of Maine was separated from Massachusetts and was admitted as a free state, and an extension of the southern border of Missouri became the new line dividing slave and free territory.

Reading the Map

1. The Mason-Dixon line, the boundary between Pennsylvania and Maryland, became the symbolic border between the original free and slave states.

2. The Ohio River functioned as a natural extension of the Mason-Dixon line and the Northwest Ordinance specified that the lands north and west of that river were to be free territories.

3. West of the Mississippi, the Missouri River turns north beyond its namesake state and would present geopolitical problems if it were to serve as the boundary between free and slave states because almost all of the western territories would have been opened for slavery. Moreover, Missouri, a slave territory from its beginning as a Spanish possession, not unexpectedly applied for admission as a slave state.

4. Looking ahead in 1821, one could expect Florida and Arkansas to become slave states, balanced by the last two free areas of the Northwest Territory: Michigan and Wisconsin. Then the balancing act would run out because the area north of the Missouri Compromise line of 36° 30′ was much greater than the land to the south.

Working with the Map

To extend their power in the Union, proponents of slavery tried on a number of occasions between 1821 and 1861 (year when the Civil War began) to alter the Missouri Compromise line. Several notable attempts were:

1. Expanding the nation southward to incorporate Mexican possessions like Texas and New Mexico as slave states;

2. Passing legislation that moved the compromise line northward;

3. Erasing the Missouri Compromise line entirely by a Supreme Court decision ruling that any restriction of the movement of private property, like slaves, was unconstitutional.

Using your American history textbook for reference and the map as a guide, write a short essay that adds historical detail to the outline above.

The Transportation Revolution: Roads and Canals, 1820–1850

Maptalk

The titles of maps are instructive. Here the story is the transportation revolution of the three decades after 1820. But the colon indicates that this particular map will only deal with part of the story, specifically roads and canals. More maps would be needed to illustrate other aspects of the transportation revolution, such as the advent of steamboats and introduction of railroads, which also occurred at this time.

In 1850 the main power on roads and canals was provided by draft animals. Oxen, horses, and mules pulled wagons, stagecoaches, packets, and barges. The introduction of steam locomotives on railroad tracks and steamboats on rivers advanced the revolution with more vigor, but this map does a good job in showing how even using only animal power, roads and canals tied the various states together with a national transportation system.

Reading the Map

1. The National Road was originally called the Cumberland Road because it was designed to link the Maryland city at the head of the Potomac River valley with the Ohio River. This road across the mountains was the first major internal improvement or public works project funded by the federal government. Congress passed the bill in 1806, construction began in 1811 and the road was in operation by 1818.

2. The Cumberland Road became known as the National Road when various extensions pushed it to the capital cities of Ohio, Indiana, and Illinois, but it never reached its goal, the Mississippi River across from St. Louis.

3. The Erie Canal across New York State opened in 1825, after eight years of construction. By providing a water link between the Hudson River and the Great Lakes, the Erie channeled the produce of the Midwest into the port of New York.

4. The success of the Erie Canal set off a wave of canal digging in the United States. Pennsylvania tried to imitate its neighbor and all of the states north of the Ohio River used canals to connect the Great Lakes with the Mississippi River system.

5. The old Boston Post Road, which in colonial times extended from Boston to Williamsburg, Virginia, was extended all the way to Florida by 1850.

Working with the Map

After studying the map, consult your textbook and other reference books as needed to match the following key city in 1850 with the road or canal that contributed to its growth.

_____ 1. Chicago   A. East Coast Post Road

_____ 2. Baltimore   B. Miami and Erie Canal

_____ 3. Nashville   C. Cumberland Road

_____ 4. Buffalo   D. Illinois and Michigan Canal

_____ 5. Cincinnati   E. Natchez Trace

_____ 6. Columbus   F. Erie Canal

_____ 7. Jacksonville G. National Road

The Removal of Native Americans, 1820–1843

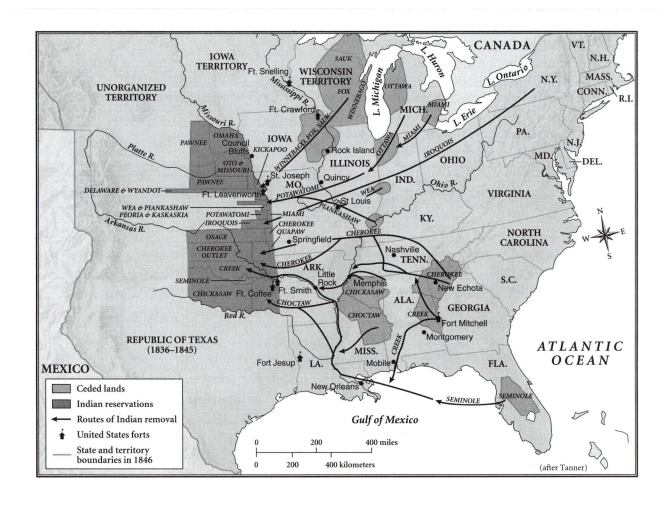

Maptalk

In American society maps tend to have an optimistic quality. We consult them for travel arrangements, like vacations and sometimes to pursue work opportunities. They suggest movement, change, and development, set into a positive context by Americans' orientation to a better tomorrow. But this map is different.

The title seems innocuous when it speaks of "removal," but the situation becomes clear when we glance at the key and read about "forced migration routes." Students are often disturbed to read about this tragedy of Native American loss and alienation, an important part of the historical record during a time that was so full of optimism, expectation, and triumph.

Reading the Map

1. The overall goal of national policy during this period was the removal of Native American peoples from their ancestral lands east of the Mississippi to large tracts of "vacant" lands on the Great Plains. Many Americans felt that white and Indian societies could not exist side by side.

2. Some maps published during this period label a broad swath of land north of Texas as a great Indian reserve. On this map the reserve is divided into rectangular tracts, each one assigned to a different tribe.

3. The map shows the various removal routes to new reservations. In these routes, Native Americans were forced to travel with army escorts. Most of these were long treks over land, but in one case a sea route was used.

4. At this time there were no bridges across the Mississippi and crossing the river was a major task in the exodus of the tribes. The crossing often involved hardship and death. Several historical parks now commemorate these crossing sites.

5. Crossing the Mississippi, then as now, was a psychological experience as well as a geographic movement. In the minds of many Americans, the "Great River" divided the "Wild West" from the older west and settled east. In the majority view, Native Americans belonged in the wilds, not in civilized society.

Working with the Map

This map looks complicated because it includes many tribes and a variety of routes. Even so, it is selective and many branches of the routes of removal are not shown. One way to understand the map is to focus on one tribe and trace its route from homeland to reservation. Select a tribe and research some details about this particular forced migration and develop a paragraph entitled "One People's Experience" to serve as the caption for this map.

The Underground Railroad in the 1850s

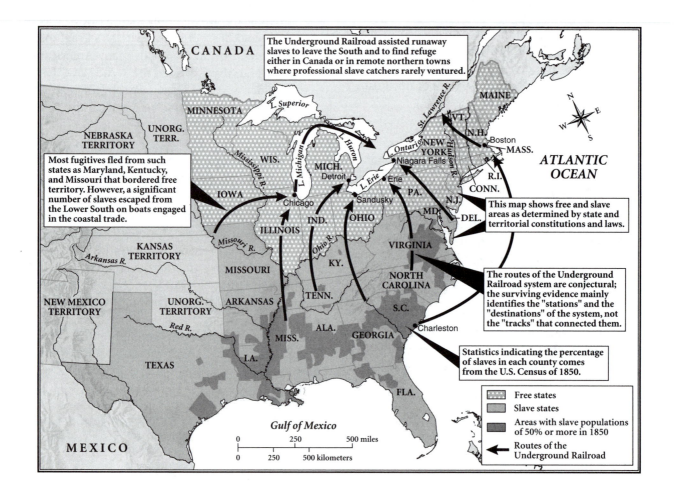

The Underground Railroad assisted runaway slaves to leave the South and to find refuge either in Canada or in remote northern towns where professional slave catchers rarely ventured.

Most fugitives fled from such states as Maryland, Kentucky, and Missouri that bordered free territory. However, a significant number of slaves escaped from the Lower South on boats engaged in the coastal trade.

This map shows free and slave areas as determined by state and territorial constitutions and laws.

The routes of the Underground Railroad system are conjectural; the surviving evidence mainly identifies the "stations" and the "destinations" of the system, not the "tracks" that connected them.

Statistics indicating the percentage of slaves in each county comes from the U.S. Census of 1850.

Free states
Slave states
Areas with slave populations of 50% or more in 1850
Routes of the Underground Railroad

Gulf of Mexico

0   250   500 miles
0   250   500 kilometers

Maptalk

The verb "to map" sometimes designates a process clarifying a course of action by employing symbols or images to create a graphic design. To map, in this sense, is to reveal something that seems to be hidden or too abstract to be easily understood. When people map out their future, they frequently create a plan for a career. Elements that could not be seen at the beginning then become clear.

A map of the Underground Railroad reveals something that was hidden in its own time. In the decades before the Civil War, the Underground Railroad was a secret network of routes and hiding places along which antislavery people helped slaves escape from the South to freedom in a free state or Canada. The network was known by word of mouth rather than by maps or written directions. No one really knew the system in its entirety.

Historians try to reconstruct the Underground Railroad by studying diaries, letters, and reminiscences. Individual parts of the network have been outlined with some authority, but the institution as a whole is very difficult to document. This particular map must be viewed as a general reconstruction rather than as a detailed map with precise locations and specific dates. It is estimated that approximately 100,000 slaves reached freedom by way of the Underground Railroad between 1793, the date of the first Fugitive Slave Act, and 1861, the start of the Civil War.

Reading the Map

1. Ohio was probably the most active state in the Underground Railroad because it offered the shortest route to Canada, had a long southern boundary facing several slave states, and had many effective leaders who helped slaves to escape.

2. In Canada escaped slaves established communities immediately north of Lake Erie. A line drawn between Detroit and Niagara Falls would indicate the general area of those settlements.

3. Chicago, Illinois; Sandusky, Ohio; and Erie, Pennsylvania were all important ports on the Great Lakes where fugitives hid on board lake boats and successfully made the trip to Canada.

4. Most of the "passengers" on the Underground Railroad started their journey in upper South states like Kentucky, Virginia, and Maryland. Slaves in the Deep South had a long journey through slave territory without help from the "conductors." One hope for a fugitive in the Deep South was to reach a port city and try to escape as a stowaway on a ship taking a route like the one marked on the map from Charleston, South Carolina, to New England.

5. In Canada, the province of Ontario was the primary destination of escaped slaves. On one day in 1850 almost 300 slaves made good their escape into Canada by crossing the Detroit River.

Working with the Map

Two famous passengers on the Underground Railroad were Frederick Douglass and Harriet Tubman. Consult your textbook or other reference books for more information about these two individuals and then write a brief summary of one of their lives, using the map as the basis of your biographical sketch.

The Mexican Cession, 1848–1853

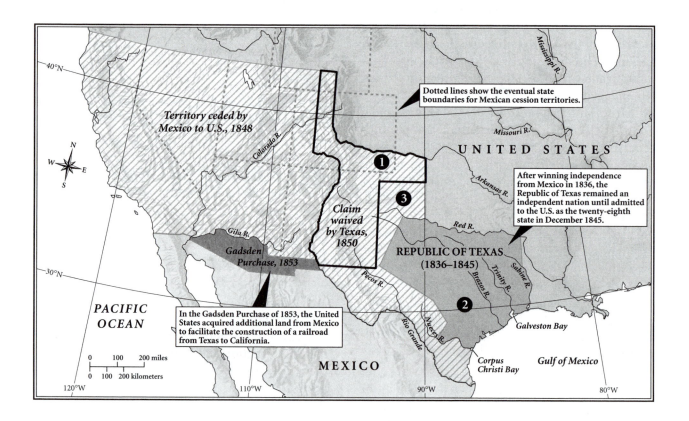

Territory ceded by
Mexico to U.S., 1848

Dotted lines show the eventual state
boundaries for Mexican cession territories.

UNITED STATES

After winning independence
from Mexico in 1836, the
Republic of Texas remained an
independent nation until admitted
to the U.S. as the twenty-eighth
state in December 1845.

Claim
waived
by Texas,
1850

Gadsden
Purchase, 1853

REPUBLIC OF TEXAS
(1836–1845)

PACIFIC
OCEAN

In the Gadsden Purchase of 1853, the United
States acquired additional land from Mexico
to facilitate the construction of a railroad
from Texas to California.

MEXICO

Galveston Bay

Corpus
Christi Bay

Gulf of Mexico

0   100   200 miles
0   100   200 kilometers

Mississippi R.
Missouri R.
Arkansas R.
Red R.
Colorado R.
Gila R.
Pecos R.
Rio Grande
Nueces R.
Brazos R.
Trinity R.
Sabine R.

120°W   110°W   90°W   80°W
40°N   30°N

Maptalk

This map shows the Republic of Texas, which became a state in 1845, and the Mexican cession territories of 1848 and 1853. This entire region is often called the American Southwest. For the Mexicans and the Americans of this period, these vast northern territories, lightly settled at the time, posed a challenge to govern because of the great distances from the central government.

On maps, distances are indicated by a scale, like the one in the lower left of this map. On the projection used in this map, distance is shown in both the English and metric systems of measurement. In most map projections, the scale varies slightly from one part of the map to another. Thus the scale often represents an average or typical measure. On some maps the scale is given as a ratio or fraction, indicating the relationship between one unit on the map to the actual distance on the ground. In this particular map, the ratio is about 1:20,000,000. One inch on the map thus represents 20 million inches in reality.

Reading the Map

1. There are three categories of land shown on this map. First there are the territories that in 1848 were indisputably part of the United States. Second there are the lands that remained part of Mexico after 1853. The other lands fall into a third classification: territory in dispute or which changed hands between 1848 and 1853.

2. Texas is also divided into three categories. The largest parcel (1) represents the claim that the new republic advanced in 1836. The smallest unit (2) shows the territory recognized by Mexico when Texas became part of the United States. The middle-size Texas (3) is roughly the same as today's state, its boundaries having been extended as a result of the Mexican War and then cut back as part of the Compromise of 1850.

3. The United States and Great Britain claimed the land north of the Mexican Cession of 1848 called Oregon. Both nations agreed to a policy of joint occupation in 1818. By peaceful agreement in 1846, American and Britain set the 49th parallel as the boundary between American Oregon and British Columbia.

4. Note that the dotted lines on the map show the states that were created out of former Mexican lands.

Working with the Map

To become familiar with the extent of the territory acquired in 1848 from Mexico in the treaty of Guadalupe-Hidalgo, label on this map all the states created from the Mexican cessions. Consult your textbook or other historical references to find the date of admission for each one, then record these dates on the map.

The Conquest of the South, 1861–1865

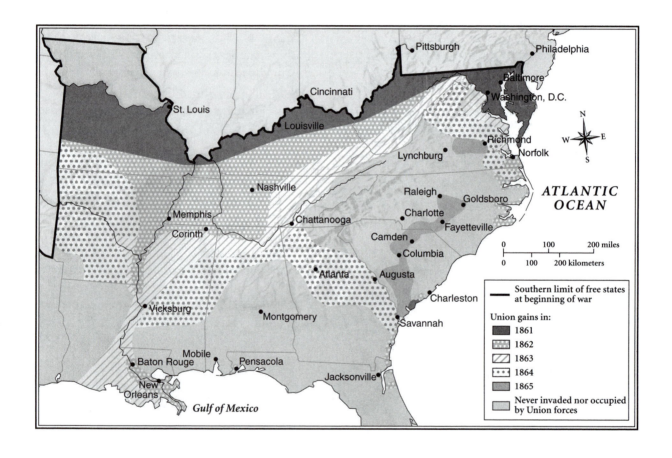

Maptalk

Titles are always important for maps and this one is particularly striking. Other possible titles might read "The Crushing of the Great Rebellion," or "The War for Southern Independence," or simply "The Civil War." Each wording carries a different meaning both in terms of the actual words used (the denotation) and also the historical associations that the particular words convey (the connotation).

The Latin root word of "conquest" originally meant to procure, that is to get something by special effort. In a conquest, something new is acquired at another's expense, often by force as was the case in the United States Civil War. After five years of warfare, the North "acquired" the surrender of the South and slavery was abolished.

The victory of the North in 1865 changed circumstances for the victor as well as the vanquished. Historians have pointed out that in the Civil War, claims of absolute state sovereignty, whether from the North or the South, could no longer be sustained in the face of the growing power in the federal government. An old two-volume textbook put it this way: American history before 1865 was the story of "The Federal Union." After 1865 the title changed to "The American Nation." With this in mind, the connotation of "conquest" in the title of this map might be extended. The Northern states, as states, also lost out to the forces of centralization and nationalism.

Reading the Map

1. The map shows how military forces from the North invaded and gradually occupied the territory of the slave states between 1861 and 1865. The starting point is shown as the Mason-Dixon line between Pennsylvania and Maryland, the Ohio River, and the Missouri Compromise lines.

2. Note that the state of West Virginia is included on this map. The western counties of Virginia refused to join in seceding from the Union and then organized themselves as a separate state, which gained admission to the U.S. in 1863 as the 35th state.

3. The map shows the importance of the Mississippi in the course of the war. The river became the fault line along which the Confederacy split into two parts. Union troops invaded south from Illinois as well as north from the Gulf of Mexico, meeting at Vicksburg in the summer of 1863.

4. Because this map depicts the situation at the end of each calendar year, it does not show the ebb and flow of troop movements, especially the Confederate invasion of Pennsylvania that was stopped at Gettysburg in July 1863.

5. The two states which saw a disproportionate amount of the fighting were Virginia and Tennessee. Both witnessed armies marching back and forth across the states as they participated in numerous campaigns.

Working with the Map

Many important cities are located on this map, but the key battles are not. Use the maps in your textbook to record the sites of these crucial events. Work in chronological order and write the dates alongside the place names on the map.

1. The firing on Fort Sumter, April 1861
2. The First Battle of Bull Run, July 1861
3. New Orleans taken May 1862
4. Memphis occupied, June 1862
5. Battle of Antietam, September 1862
6. Fall of Vicksburg, July 1863
7. Battle of Gettysburg, July 1863
8. Burning of Atlanta, September 1864
9. Sherman's March to the Sea, November–December 1864
10. Battle of Petersburg, April 1865
11. Surrender at Appomattox, April 1865

WORKSHEET 15
The Barrow Plantation, 1860 and 1881

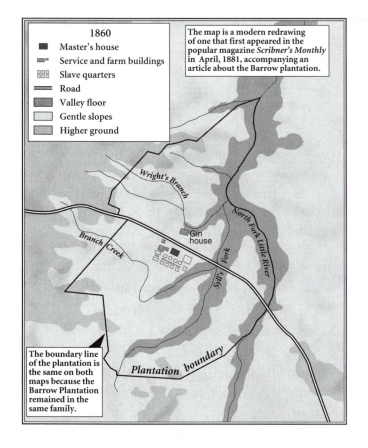

1860

- Master's house
- Service and farm buildings
- Slave quarters
- Road
- Valley floor
- Gentle slopes
- Higher ground

The map is a modern redrawing of one that first appeared in the popular magazine *Scribner's Monthly* in April, 1881, accompanying an article about the Barrow plantation.

Wright's Branch

Branch Creek

Gin house

North Fork Little River

Sytl's Fork

The boundary line of the plantation is the same on both maps because the Barrow Plantation remained in the same family.

Plantation boundary

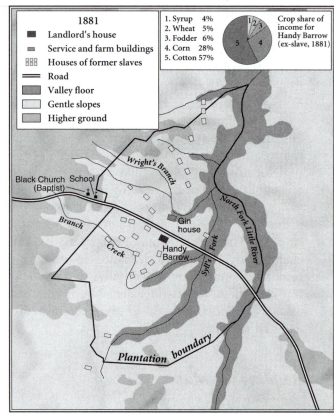

1881

- Landlord's house
- Service and farm buildings
- Houses of former slaves
- Road
- Valley floor
- Gentle slopes
- Higher ground

1. Syrup   4%
2. Wheat   5%
3. Fodder   6%
4. Corn   28%
5. Cotton 57%

Crop share of income for Handy Barrow (ex-slave, 1881)

Black Church (Baptist)   School

Wright's Branch

Branch Creek

Gin house

Handy Barrow

North Fork Little River

Sytl's Fork

Plantation boundary

Maptalk

These maps attract the student of American history for a variety of reasons. First, they are large-scale maps in which the ratio of area on the maps to area on the ground is large enough to show individual features on the landscape: houses, schools, churches, and the like. Second, the maps are of interest because they show change over time. What was the impact of freedom on a community of slaves who became sharecroppers after emancipation? A popular magazine, *Scribner's Monthly,* raised this question in 1881. The pair of maps shown here first appeared as an illustration in that article. Third, students of history will also appreciate the notes on the map. These are often referred to as "call-outs," as if a guide were calling out explanations on a field trip.

One of the challenges of a large-scale map is to place the location into a larger geographical context. Sometimes this is done by an inset map, which indicates the featured location on a map of a much smaller scale. These maps do not have such a feature, but the names of the rivers are useful in establishing the Barrow Plantation's location.

Reading the Map

1. To establish a sense of the scale of this map, the house of the master or landlord is about three-fourths of a mile from Syll's Fork or about a mile and a quarter from the 1881 church.

2. The relative location of the Barrow Plantation is about 18 miles west of Washington, Georgia and about 12 miles north of today's Interstate Route 20, which connects Atlanta with Augusta.

3. These maps are oriented by the road, which generally runs north and south rather than by the cardinal directions. Thus east is at the top of this map and the North Fork of the Little River flows from the west to the east.

4. The Barrow Plantation is located in Oglethorpe County, named after the founder of Georgia.

5. Note that the maps show no houses immediately below (northwest of) Branch Creek. This low-lying area was covered with forest in 1860 as well as 1881, but soon thereafter a patch was cleared upstream along Syll's Fork to accommodate several new houses and fields.

Working with the Map

The changes recorded in the 1881 map probably did not happen at the same time. A third map, dated 1868 or 1870, might have recorded a transition from one pattern of settlement to another. Trace the major geographic features from one of these maps onto a new sheet of paper. Then develop a hypothetical map of the Barrow Plantation midway through the transition stage, say about 1869. Write two or three callouts for this new map explaining the changes in motion.

SECTION THREE

One-Minute Map Quizzes

The Spanish Encounter with Native Americans

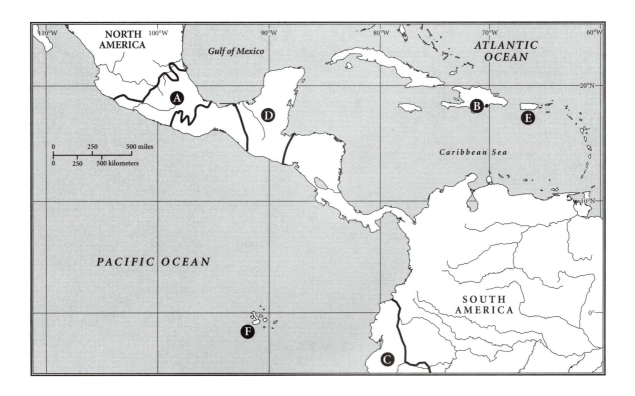

Choose the letter on the map that correctly identifies each of the following:

_____ 1. Aztec empire

_____ 2. Mayan empire

_____ 3. Santo Domingo

_____ 4. Inca empire

_____ 5. Puerto Rico

The Puritan Migration to America, 1620–1640

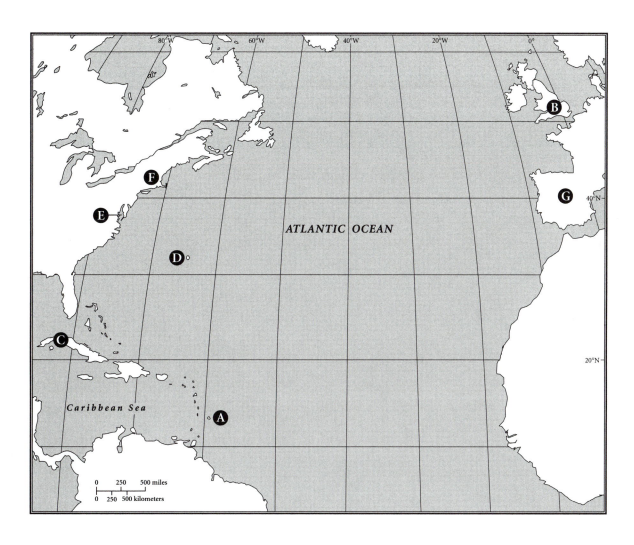

Choose the letter on the map that correctly identifies each of the following:

_____ 1. England

_____ 2. New England

_____ 3. Bermuda

_____ 4. Chesapeake Bay

_____ 5. Barbados

QUIZ 3

Britain's American Empire, 1713

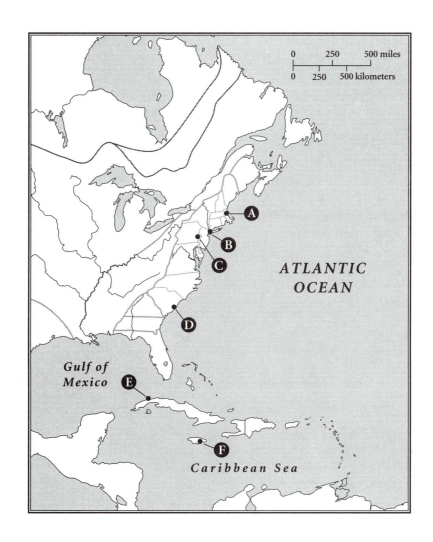

Choose the letter on the map that correctly identifies each of the following:

_____ 1. Boston

_____ 2. New York

_____ 3. Kingston

_____ 4. Charleston

_____ 5. Philadelphia

European Spheres of Influence, 1754

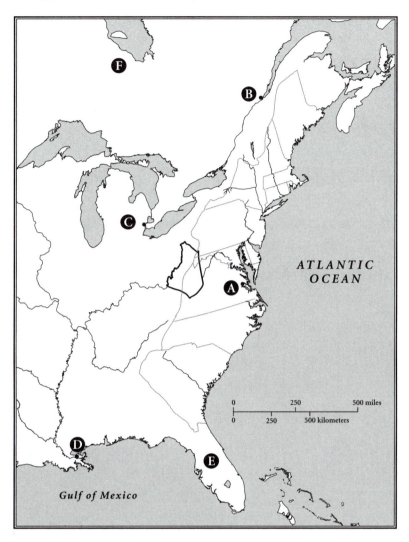

Locate the following on the map and identify the country that claimed it in 1754:

_____	_____	1. Florida
_____	_____	2. Quebec
_____	_____	3. Williamsburg
_____	_____	4. New Orleans
_____	_____	5. Hudson's Bay Company

QUIZ 5
British America, 1763–1775

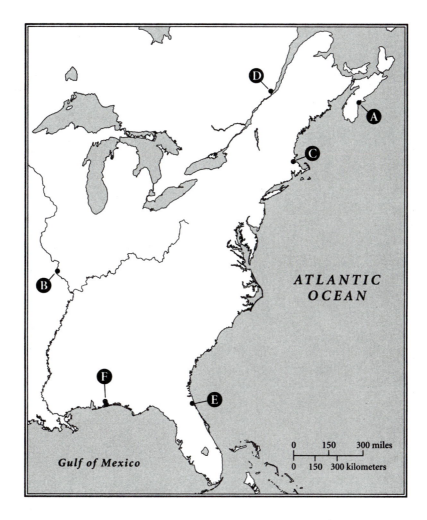

Choose the letter on the map that correctly identifies each of the following:

_____ 1. Boston

_____ 2. St. Augustine

_____ 3. Quebec

_____ 4. Pensacola

_____ 5. Halifax

The War for Independence, 1775–1783

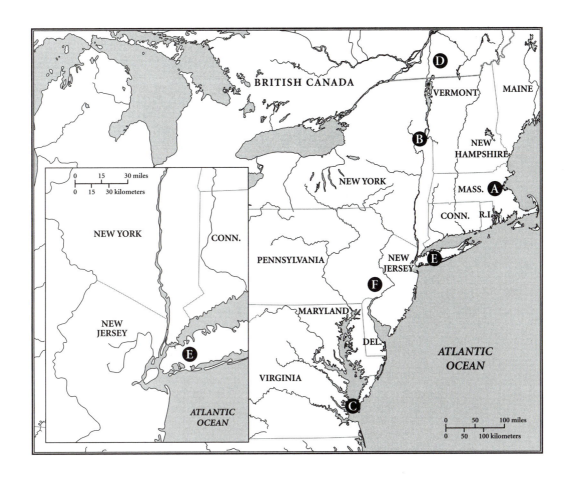

Choose the letter on the map that correctly identifies each of the following:

_____ 1. Saratoga

_____ 2. Bunker Hill

_____ 3. Valley Forge

_____ 4. Yorktown

_____ 5. Long Island

QUIZ 7
Ratifying the Constitution of 1787

Choose the letter on the map that correctly identifies each of the following:

_____ 1. First state to ratify the Constitution

_____ 2. State where Patrick Henry "smelled a rat"

_____ 3. The last of the original thirteen states to ratify the Constitution

_____ 4. Alexander Hamilton represented this state at the Constitutional convention

_____ 5. Shays's Rebellion

Native American Frontier, 1789–1820

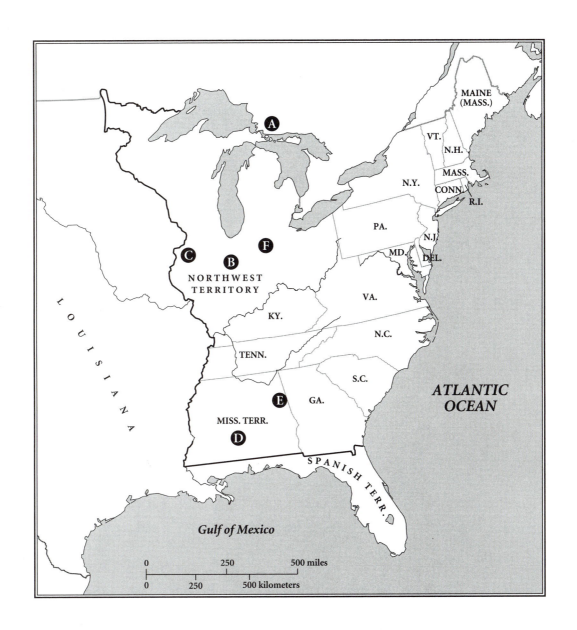

Choose the letter on the map that correctly identifies each of the following:

_____ 1. Site of the Battle of Tippecanoe

_____ 2. Black Hawk's home territory

_____ 3. Site of St. Clair's defeat

_____ 4. Creek native lands

_____ 5. Choctaw native lands

The Missouri Compromise, 1820–1821

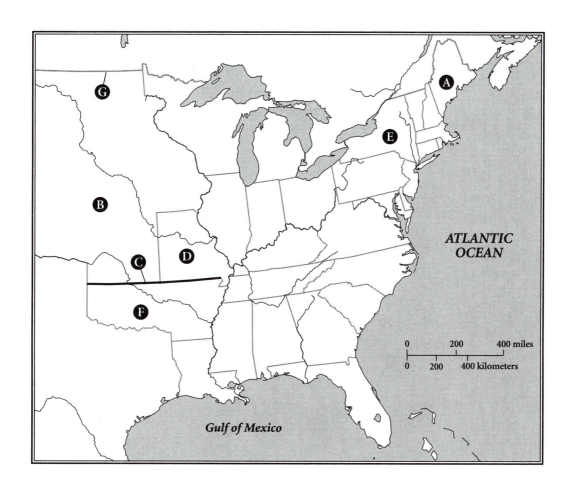

Choose the letter on the map that correctly identifies each of the following:

_____ 1. Missouri Compromise line

_____ 2. Maine, admitted 1820

_____ 3. Missouri, admitted 1821

_____ 4. Area opened to slavery by the Missouri Compromise

_____ 5. Area closed to slavery by the Missouri Compromise

The Transportation Revolution: Roads and Canals, 1820–1850

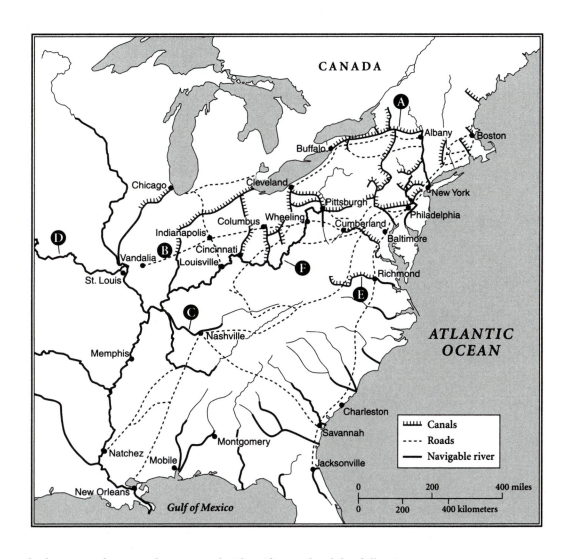

Choose the letter on the map that correctly identifies each of the following:

_____ 1. The Erie Canal

_____ 2. The National Road

_____ 3. The Ohio River

_____ 4. The Missouri River

_____ 5. The James River Canal

The United States in 1830: National Leaders

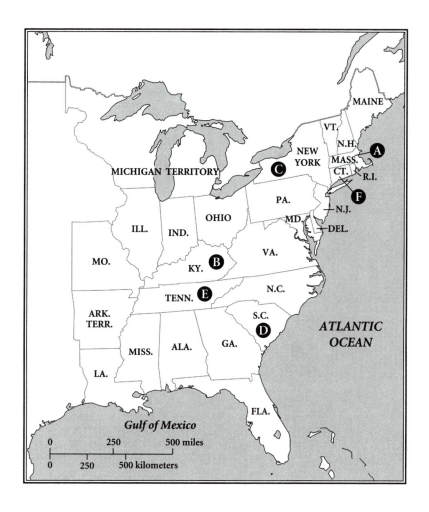

Choose the letter on the map that correctly identifies the home state of each of the following political leaders:

_____ 1. Andrew Jackson

_____ 2. John C. Calhoun

_____ 3. Martin Van Buren

_____ 4. Henry Clay

_____ 5. John Quincy Adams

Major Communal Experiments before 1860

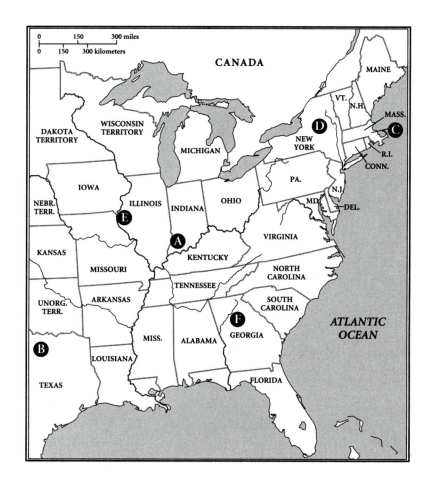

Choose the letter on the map that correctly identifies each of the following:

_____ 1. New Harmony

_____ 2. Oneida Community

_____ 3. Brook Farm

_____ 4. Icaria

_____ 5. Nauvoo

Settlement of the Trans-Missouri West, 1835–1860

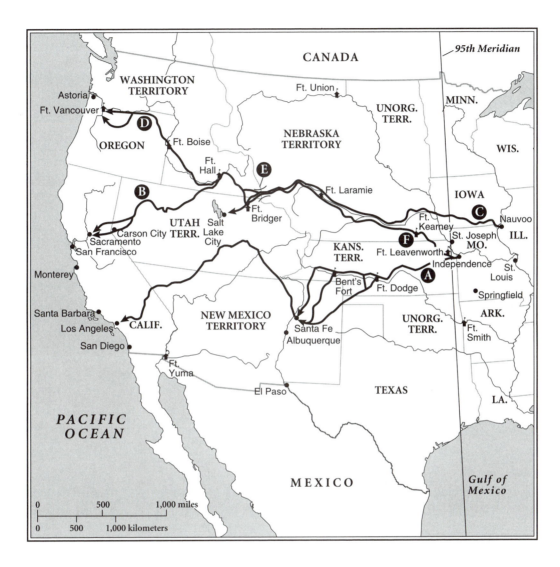

Choose the letter on the map that correctly identifies each of the following:

_____ 1. Mormon Trail

_____ 2. Santa Fe Trail

_____ 3. Oregon Trail

_____ 4. California Trail

_____ 5. South Pass

The Civil War in Virginia, 1864–1865

Choose the letter on the map that correctly identifies each of the following:

_____ 1. The Wilderness

_____ 2. Spotsylvania

_____ 3. Petersburg

_____ 4. Richmond

_____ 5. Appomattox Court House

QUIZ 15
Reconstruction, 1865–1877

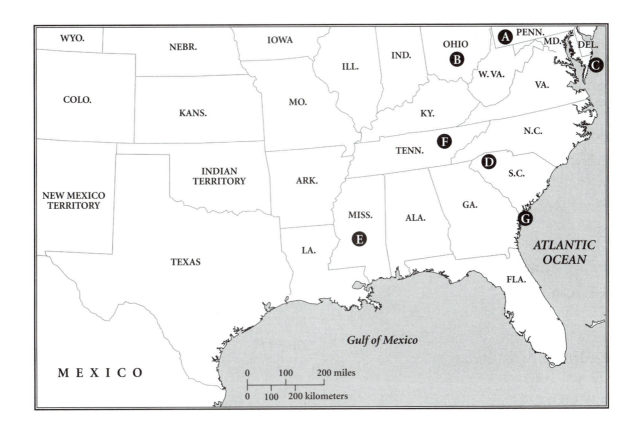

Choose the letter on the map that correctly identifies each of the following:

_____ 1. First former Confederate state readmitted to the Union, 1866

_____ 2. Area of sea islands and coastal plantations where General Sherman
settled freedmen on 40-acre tracts, 1865

_____ 3. Home state of Radical Republican Thaddeus Stevens

_____ 4. State that sent Hiram R. Revels to the U.S. Senate as its first African
American member, 1890

_____ 5. Home state of Republican Party presidential candidate Rutherford B.
Hayes, 1876

Answer Key

Basic Geography

Worksheet C
1-G, 2-E, 3-F, 4-J, 5-H, 6-C, 7-D, 8-I, 9-B, 10-A

Worksheet D
1-H, 2-D, 3-G, 4-B, 5-E, 6-C, 7-A, 8-I, 9-F, 10-J

Mapping America's History

Worksheet 10
1.D, 2.C, 3.E, 4.F, 5.B, 6.G, 7.A

One-Minute Map Quizzes

Quiz 1
1.A, 2.D, 3.B, 4.C, 5.E

Quiz 2
1.B, 2.F, 3.D, 4.E, 5.A

Quiz 3
1.A, 2.B, 3.F, 4.D, 5.C

Quiz 4
1.E-Spain, 2.B-France, 3.A-Britain, 4.D-France, 5.F-Britain

Quiz 5
1.C, 2.E, 3.D, 4.F, 5.A

Quiz 6
1.B, 2.A, 3.F, 4.C, 5.E

Quiz 7
1.A, 2.C, 3.F, 4.B, 5.D

Quiz 8
1.F, 2.C, 3.B, 4.E, 5.D

Quiz 9
1.C, 2.A, 3.D, 4.F, 5.B

Quiz 10
1.A, 2.B, 3.F, 4.D, 5.E

Quiz 11
1.E, 2.D, 3.C, 4.B, 5.A

Quiz 12
1.A, 2.D, 3.C, 4.B, 5.E

Quiz 13
1.C, 2.A, 3.D, 4.B, 5.E

Quiz 14
1.A, 2.B, 3.C, 4.D, 5.F

Quiz 15
1.F, 2.G, 3.A, 4.E, 5.B

Outline Reference Maps

North America: Physical Geography

The United States: Political Divisions

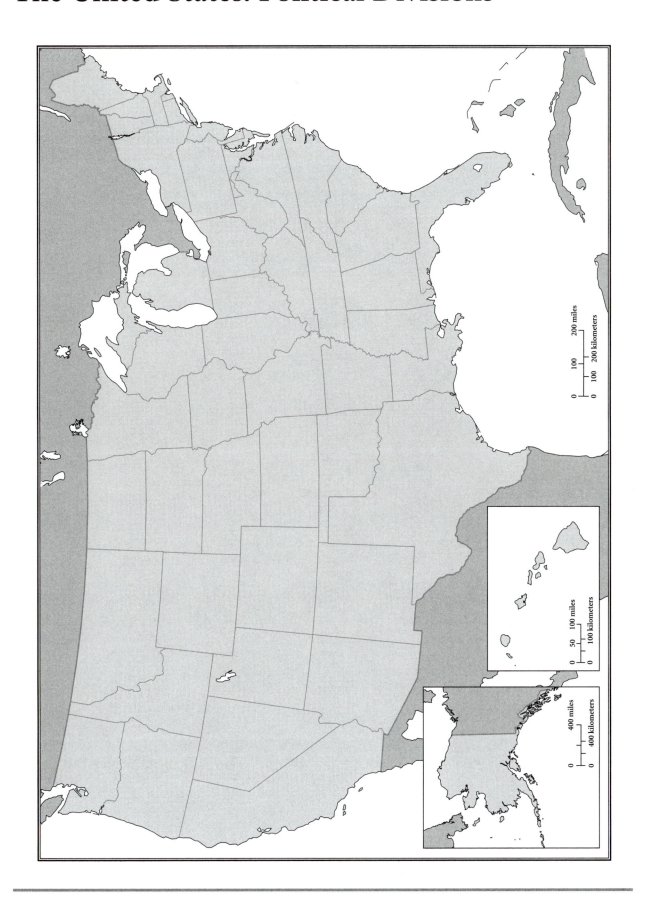

The World: Physical Geography

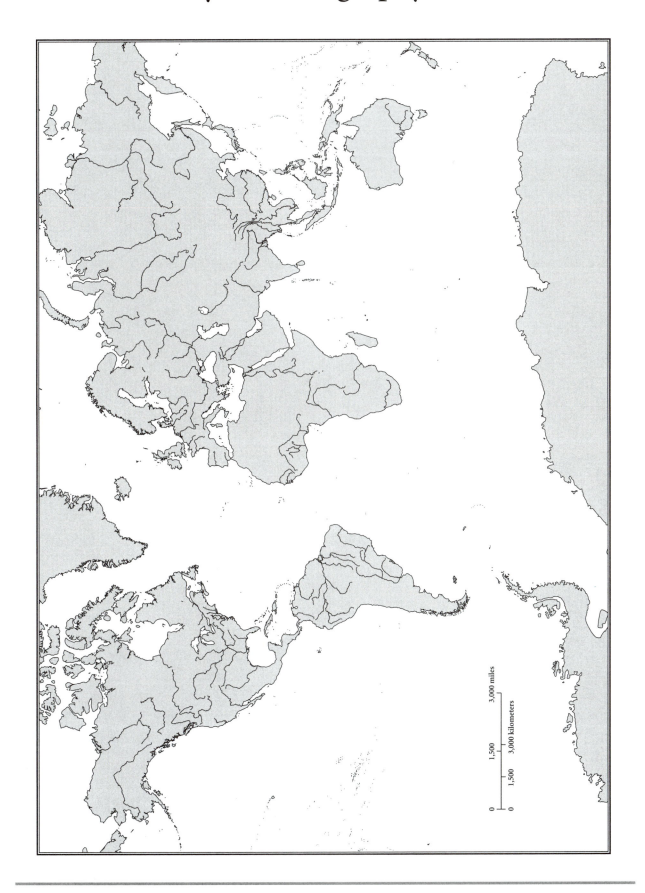

3,000 miles

1,500

3,000 kilometers

1,500

0

0

The World: Political Divisions, 2003

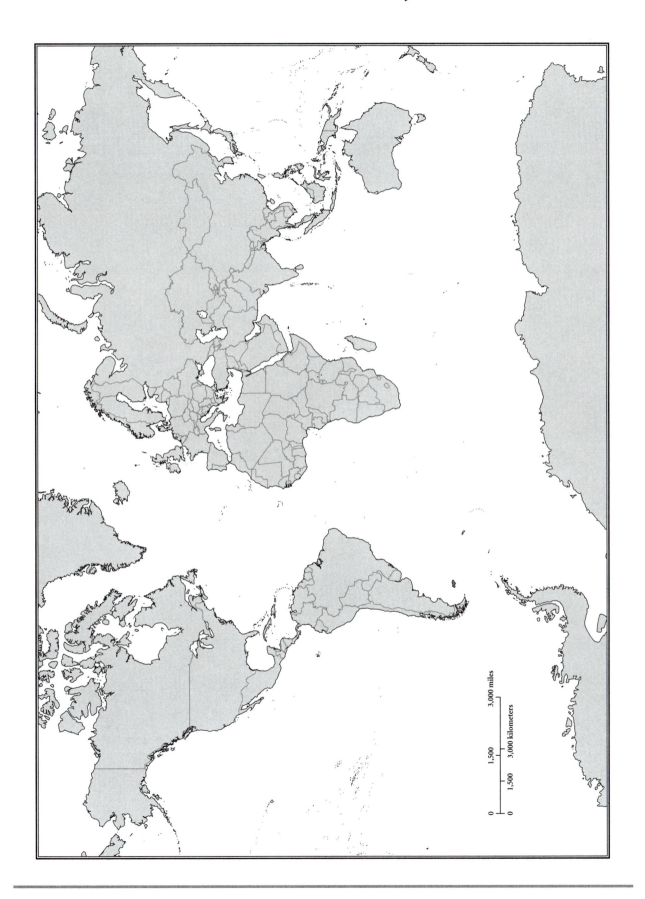

3,000 miles

1,500

3,000 kilometers

1,500

1,500

0

0